2004 POETR

ONCE UPON A RHYME

IMAGINATION FOR
A NEW GENERATION

Devon & Cornwall
Edited by Steve Twelvetree

 Young**Writers**

First published in Great Britain in 2004 by:
Young Writers
Remus House
Coltsfoot Drive
Peterborough
PE2 9JX
Telephone: 01733 890066
Website: www.youngwriters.co.uk

SB ISBN 1 84460 546 9

Foreword

Young Writers was established in 1991 and has been passionately devoted to the promotion of reading and writing in children and young adults ever since. The quest continues today. Young Writers remains as committed to engendering the fostering of burgeoning poetic and literary talent as ever.

This year's Young Writers competition has proven as vibrant and dynamic as ever and we are delighted to present a showcase of the best poetry from across the UK. Each poem has been carefully selected from a wealth of *Once Upon A Rhyme* entries before ultimately being published in this, our twelfth primary school poetry series.

Once again, we have been supremely impressed by the overall high quality of the entries we have received. The imagination, energy and creativity which has gone into each young writer's entry made choosing the best poems a challenging and often difficult but ultimately hugely rewarding task - the general high standard of the work submitted amply vindicating this opportunity to bring their poetry to a larger appreciative audience.

We sincerely hope you are pleased with our final selection and that you will enjoy *Once Upon A Rhyme Devon & Cornwall* for many years to come.

Contents

Bolham CP School, Tiverton

Gemma Cotter (9)	17
Bethany Lane (9)	18
Sophie Hill (9)	19
Holly Drew (9)	20
Ellen Howe (10)	20
Douglas Pullar (10)	21
William Luxton (10)	21
Edward Pullar (7)	22

Braunton Caen CP School, Braunton

Michael Bevan (11)	23
Marcus Lywood (11)	23
Aydan Greatrick (10)	24
Rachel Sandy (10)	24
Jasmine Whiteleaf (10)	25
Jake Edwards (10)	25
Rhiannon Jewell (10)	25
Hayley Swann (11)	26
Victoria Pennington (11)	26
Josh Murray (11)	26
Kelly Swann (11)	27
Charlotte Hart (10)	27
Izzy Brookes (10)	28
Libby Wastie (11)	28
Jenny Coles (11)	29
Liam Allman (10)	29
Phoebe Reed (11)	30

Coads Green Primary School, Launceston

Sam Gardiner (10)	30
Sammy Wheeler (10)	31
Rosanna Dinnis (10)	32
Elizabeth Hosking (9)	32
Ben Berger (11)	33
Carly Halls (10)	34
Jordan James (10)	35
Ben Norgate (11)	35
Isabel Brumwell (10)	36
James Goodman (9)	37

Fourlanesend CP School, Torpoint

Ralph Arscott (10)	37
Maizey Peters (11)	38
Joshua Willcocks (11)	38
Tom Kendall (11)	39
Thomas Calladine (11)	39
Lisa Marie Baker (11)	40
Bonnie Farley (11)	40
Darren Mitchell (10)	40
Chloe Adams (10)	41
Sam Wacher-Carne (10)	41
Lillian Rogers (9)	42
Emma Platts (10)	42
Ryan Cooper (11)	43

Hayward CP School, Crediton

Josh Pike (10)	43
Esther Thorn Gent (10)	44
Ben Reed (9)	44
Natalie Armstrong (10)	44
Jessica Bailey (9)	45
Amy Hill (9)	45
Aaron Davey (10)	45
Michelle Soper (10)	46
Charlotte Parsons (10)	46
Owaen Guppy (10)	47
Liam Lowey (10)	47
Lewis Pinn (10)	47
Stephanie Yelland (9)	48
Sean Mills (9)	48
Daniel Boddy (10)	49
Michael Raymont (10)	49
Brecon Eveleigh (10)	49
Fred Conyngham (9)	50
Lisa Chart (10)	50
Kaylee Branch (9)	51

Honiton CP School, Honiton

Arthur Sayers (11)	51
Daniel Cooke (10)	52

Aaron King (11)	81
Lydia Heaven (11)	82
Isobel Dobson (11)	83
Kirsty Sanders (10)	84
Ben Bright (11)	84
Niall Boulton (8)	85
Lauren Strutt (11)	85
Alex Gocher (10)	86
Danielle Wakley (11)	87
Shannon Croton (11)	88
Holly Ainsworth (11)	89
Laura Woollacott (8)	90
Yasmin Miller (7)	90
Amy Shawyer (7)	91
Harriet Morris (8)	91
Matthew Richards (8)	92

Ilfracombe CE Junior School, Ilfracombe

Bethany Parsons (10)	92
Fay Ackfield-Case (9)	93
Gina Bryant (9)	93
Matthew McKee (9)	94
Sofia Vicente (9)	94
Rachel Threlkeld & Beth Parsons (10)	95
Jack Turner & Daniel Barbeary (11)	95
Sarah Campbell (9)	96
Caitlin Robertson (10)	96
Katy McCarten (10)	97
Naomi Dymond-Drury (10)	97
Abigail Barter (10)	98
Ella Mawson (8)	98
Megan Barnes (8)	99
Lauren Burge (10)	99
Lee Holden (11)	100
Charlotte Campbell (11)	100
Adam Smith (10)	100
Alicia Fay (10)	101
Jordan Davey (11)	101
Emily Wells (10)	102
Kelsey Jackson (9)	102
Katrina Bryant (11)	103

Kelly Davison (10)   103
Jessica Hornsby (8)   104
Chloe Huelin (8)   104
Sophie Campbell (8)   105

Keyham Barton Catholic Primary School, Plymouth
Joseph Borthwick (9)   105
Peter Jerrett (9)   106
Niamh O'Connell (9)   107
Harvey Parsons (8)   108
Amber Seymour (9)   108
William Ashfield (9)   109

Ladock CE Primary School, Truro
Rebecca Trethewey (11)   110
Caitlin Mulroy (10)   110
Joseph Moore (11)   111

Luxulyan School, Bodmin
Ryan Goodwin (11)   111
Heather Charlesworth (10)   112
Jessica Bone (11)   112
Emily Andrews (11)   112
Steven Hooper (10)   113
Shannon Fahey (10)   113
Ashley Hick (9)   114
Eddie George (7)   114
Shaun Pickering (11)   114
Luke Rowe (10)   114
Lauren Hoskin (9)   115

Mount Charles CP School, St Austell
Jessica Haley (11)   115
Chaela Richmond (9)   115
Danny Allum (10)   116
Jamileh Clifford (10)   116
Hannah Salisbury (11)   117
Lily Richardson (8)   117
Georgia Haywood (8)   118
Sophie Marsh (7)   118

Mullion Primary School, Helston

Mark Leach (11)	138
Becky Sandford (10)	139
Hannah Richardson (11)	139

Newport Primary School, Barnstaple

Gemma Wells (8)	140
Max Banbury (8)	140
Lewis Hall (8)	141
Shivon Burridge (8)	141
Charlie Sherborne (11)	142
Naomi Straughan (9)	142
Samuel Clarke (8)	143
Melanie Thompson (8)	143
Nicholas Shanley (10)	144
Sam Hui (11)	144
Rebecca Ellis (10)	145
Nicole McBride (10)	145
Rebekah Parsons (10)	146
Abigail Tanton (11)	146
Jason Head (10)	147
Ashley Roberts (10)	147
Elisa Field (10)	148
Jessica Poile (11)	149
Eleanor Chamings (11)	149
Aaron Milne-Redhead (10)	150
Matthew Wallin (11)	150
Jessica Loder (8)	151
Charli Dellaway (9)	151
Ben Hardy (8)	152
Danyelle Snell (10)	152
Lucy Hardy (11)	153
Samuel Pincombe (8)	153
Charlotte Rushton (8)	154
Myah Field (8)	154
Jacob Harris (8)	155
Miles Kingsley (8)	155
Jason Tucker (11)	156
Bethany Westcott (8)	156
Rachel Elston (10)	157
Charlie Hedge (11)	157
Kurtis Hartnoll (10)	158

Hannah Loder (11)   159
Kelly Featherstone (10)   159
Hannah Sutton (8)   159
Jade Harris (8)   160
Liam Andrew (9)   160
Justin Southam (9)   161
Charles Rogers (9)   161
Matthew Pearson (9)   162
Jessica Smith (8)   162
Rebecca Benham (9)   163
Jamie Shutt (9)   163
Myles Payne (8)   164
Gemma Bolsom (8)   164
Thomas Roode (9)   165
Siân O'Neill (8)   165
Shane Prater (9)   166

St John's CE Primary School, Totnes
Bernadette Wreford (11)   166
Joseph Trott (11)   167
Robyn McLellan (11)   167
Mark Nicholls (11)   168
Stephen Devlin (11)   168
Jasmine Moore (11)   169
Scarlett Fagan (11)   169
Matthew Edmonds (11)   170
Abigail Robbins (11)   170
Rose Lewis (11)   171
Jamie Bevan (11)   171
Rebecca Day (11)   172
Aaron Mead (11)   172
Jemma Morris (10)   173
Aaron Spray (11)   173
Amber Bayldon (11)   174
Elisha Pusey Gale (11)   175

St Mawes Primary School, Truro
Alexandra Petrucci (10)   175
Lucy Goldsmith-Cannan (10)   176
Aidan Shaw (10)   176
Steven Green (8)   176

The Poems

I Remember . . .

Before I was born, I'd wriggle and giggle, hoping to be born.
Being told to be quiet,
But it was fun having older brothers and sisters.
My first game of tag, it was so unfair, I seemed to be always 'it'!
My first day at school, I cried and cried,
But they wouldn't let me go home.
Meeting my first ever best friend,
She sat down beside me, looking so glum.
My first tooth coming out, there was loads of blood and it stung.
Getting my first school certificate, I went bright red!
Moving house, it was really scary, I didn't know anyone else.
Starting my new school, I hid in a corner and started to cry.
Making lots of new friends, I've still got them now,
They are as bright as stars!

Caroline Lloyd (10)
Ashleigh CE Primary School , Barnstaple

The Firebird

The Land of Plenty's golden apples are disappearing,
From the Land of Plenty's glowing orchard.
The Firebird's wings flutter and swish as it swifts through the air,
Flames drift through the sky
As the Firebird speeds and rushes through the gentle, brushing
breeze to steal,
The Firebird makes Tsar very ill
As he threatens the life of the Tsar and the world,
Three brothers set off to keep their ailing father alive,
Every night the Firebird races through the dazing air,
The Firebird descends as it starts to lose its boiling flames,
The wind blows and the Firebird falls to the ground
Like a frosty snowflake,
Lord Goth finds the Firebird and revives his health.

Kayleigh McGlone (9)
Ashleigh CE Primary School, Barnstaple

And My Heart Soars

The roar of a lion,
The howl of a wolf,
The speed of a cheetah,
They speak to me.

The intelligence of a dolphin,
The strength of an ant,
The ink of an octopus,
They speak to me.

The sight of an eagle,
The power of a shark,
The tooth of a piranha,
They speak to me.

The size of a whale,
The mouth of a howler monkey,
The legs of a kangaroo,
They speak to me.

The poison of a snake,
The lifespan of a tortoise,
The wings of a golden eagle,
They speak to me.

The beak of a pelican,
The buzz of a bee,
The ears of a bat,
And my heart soars.

Sam Neve (10)
Ashleigh CE Primary School, Barnstaple

My Garden

My garden has the life of joy and happiness,
With flowers that brighten up the fields with their smiles,
And the sunshine's reflection dazzles on the river.

The tallest tree stood proud as he grew blossom,
And the owl inside it tooted a happy tune,
The mysterious fairies came out for the summer,
And the mermaid sings on the soft seabed.

The phoenix flew overhead,
Sparks came out as he flew by in the sunset,
As the dragon slept in his lonely cave,
His scales glisten in the moonlight.

The stars dance all night long,
Lighting up people's lives as they slept peacefully,
And as the unicorn flew swiftly in the sky,
Making the sky look unreal.

When the sun finally rose,
The phoenix sparked a smile on the sun,
And as the dolphins leapt out of the water,
A smile showed excitement and joy.

That's what's in my garden,
A mysterious world,
A world of dreams.

Charlie Griffiths (10)
Ashleigh CE Primary School, Barnstaple

Things That My Mum Loves

Hundreds of glasses of sparkling champagne,
Brand new clothes with prices insane,
Jewellery covered from her head to her toes,
Beautiful flowery bed covers and settee throws,
Cute little puppies with pea-green eyes,
Juicy fat fish with greasy French fries,
Glamorous, fluffy, pure white doves,
These are some things that my mum loves.

Enya Garrett (10)
Ashleigh CE Primary School, Barnstaple

The Seasons Of The Year

I love spring and summer,
When all the beautiful plants grow.
I love autumn when the leaves on the trees go red and gold,
And the fruit is ripe and juicy.
But when winter comes and all the plants die,
I feel like I'm one of them,
Like I'm fading away until spring comes again.

Jay O'Rourke (10)
Berrynarbor Primary School, Ilfracombe

All About Nature

Nature, the trees, the colours, the flowers
With all very special powers.
The blue bluebells
Blossomed with lovely smells.
The bad stinging nettles
Have not attractive petals.
Poppies, their petals bright red
Found right on a grassy bed.

Samuel Bowden (10)
Berrynarbor Primary School, Ilfracombe

Nature

I am a leaf.
I was born on a lovely blossom tree.
I sit here night and day.
I watch the flowers come to life.
Watching the squirrels collect their nuts
For winter to come.

At night I can see the moon shining on me.
Listen to the creatures of the night.
As I watch the birds in their nests
I start to fall and I drift peacefully to the ground.

Winter has come!

Stacey Hale (10)
Berrynarbor Primary School, Ilfracombe

Countryside

Walking in the countryside,
Smelling the fresh new flowers.
The smell I cannot describe,
They stand like coloured towers.

The irritating nettles,
Where butterflies lay their eggs.
They have no pretty petals,
Brushing and stinging your legs.

The great colour of bluebells,
Swaying in the cool spring breeze.
The mix of the fresh spring smells,
I hear buzzing, it must be bees.

William Matthews (10)
Berrynarbor Primary School, Ilfracombe

Baby Crying

Baby crying because . . .
Barney's video has finished
All the time the baby's crying
The baby's crying
I'm sick of it
I just can't stand it.

Baby crying, baby crying because . . .
The toy has gone missing
So the baby's crying
I cannot stand it
Just cannot sleep
I have to wear earmuffs.

Just help me
Why can't you help me?
Just help me

The baby's crying because . . .
Dad is watching football
Run for your life
The pain of my ears!

But sometimes it is OK because . . .
She is happy and I like that
I like, I like that
Because she is happy
And that is the way it should be.

And I like that
I do, I do,
Yes, I do, yes, I do
Even though she cries I still love her
I still love her
So why don't you listen more closely?
I love her.

George Gray (8)
Berrynarbor Primary School, Ilfracombe

The Sea

The sea is rough,
The sea is smooth,
The sea is big,
The sea is wide.

The sea is blue,
The sea is green,
The sea is big,
The sea is wide.

I stand in the sea,
It's as cold as ice.
I ran back out,
I ran back in.
I dare to swim,
I promise I will.
The sea is big,
The sea is wide.

The fishes swim,
They're scared of you.
If you try to catch them,
They scutter away.
The sea is big,
The sea is wide.

The sea is loud,
The sea is clear.
There's more sea than land,
Land around you,
Land around you,
Sea round you.
The sea is big,
The sea is wide.

Gracie Davis (10)
Berrynarbor Primary School, Ilfracombe

The First Crack Of Spring

The first dew drop of dawn
Falls upon the shimmering lawn
The tiny dew drop bends the blade of grass
Its crystal-like form is like glass.

The wind is still gone away for yet another day
When the sun has decided not to play
Mist droops like a velvet cloth, so gentle and kind
To my face, its clearness confuses my mind.

Where the field mice sleep without a peep
And daddy long legs creep
Without a noise to be heard in this quiet place
In this kind of empty space.

A river says goodbye to passing water that will not come back again
Some day now or then it could be rain
Squadrons of fish jump off the fall
Passing the water that makes a hard wall.

The sun looks down with a smile
Meanwhile the world lives
In peace and harmony
Even squabbling geese.

Rebecca Farrell (11)
Berrynarbor Primary School, Ilfracombe

Weed

Weed, weed, you are a pest,
With you there I have no rest.
I want to dig you out,
So I can plant my seed.

I look after the plant
Day after day,
So get out of the way.

If you don't get out of my way,
I will kill you with a deadly spray.

Ross Matthews (9)
Berrynarbor Primary School, Ilfracombe

The Lonely Tree

I stand quite a way from the ground,
My leaves are smooth then prickly,
I wave to the sand as the wind drives it past me,
I watch the sea come in, go out,
Come in, go out.
I long for a friend, someone to sway with me,
Quite a way from the ground.

All I hear is the sea,
I love the sound when it crashes against the dull grey rocks.
The gulls fly, they circle over my head, perch on me,
I wish I was a bird so I could be free to go where I like,
But no,
I'm rooted deep into the ground,
I have to search deep down for my water.
It's hard being me.

Emma Vanstone (11)
Berrynarbor Primary School, Ilfracombe

The Wood Is Alive

The sun is rising over the wood
As the trees dance in the breeze
The bluebells ring like bells should
And in the cold the dew did freeze
The wood is alive.

The sun is shining on the leaves
The ladybirds like flowers standing on them
I can hear the wood breathe
Foxes cautiously come out of their den
The wood is alive.

The nettles stinging the bees in their hives
The owl hooting at its normal pace
Blades of grass looking like thousands of knives
Flies flying into the spider's lace
The wood is alive.

Lydia Maloney (11)
Berrynarbor Primary School, Ilfracombe

Springtime

In the springtime we are blessed with colours
And the sun is shining bright
All you can see is blossom that's pink
And you see them glowing at night.

The dew is fresh on the grass
And the daffodils pretty too
And when the sun is shining bright
It's always shining on you.

It looks like glitter on the grass
And crystals on the trees
You hear the singing birds
And the buzzing of the bees.

You hear the cracking of the eggs
The swishing of the trees
The calling of the birds
And herds of squabbling geese.

Then the flowers start to grow without a sound
And the mist drifts through the sky
The mice are sleeping in the long grass
It's nearly summer now, spring goodbye.

Jemma Ivan (9)
Berrynarbor Primary School, Ilfracombe

Teacher! Teacher!

Teacher! Teacher! He's fiddling with his toes.
Teacher! Teacher! She's picking her nose.
Teacher! Teacher! He's going in my den.
The acher! Teacher! She's just taken my pen.
Teacher! Teacher! He's throwing a stick.
Miss, look out, she's chucking a brick.
Teacher! Teacher! I know you don't care.
Teacher! Teacher! She's pulling my hair.
Child! Child! Watch your lip
And for goodness sake just *zip!*

Patrick Clarke (11)
Berrynarbor Primary School, Ilfracombe

Chinese Rain Dragon

Dance, dragon, dance
Make the rain come
Dance, dragon, dance
Banish the sun
Dance, dragon, dance
Beat on the drum
Try, dragon, try
To make the rain come.

The earth is dry, dragon
Crops will die, dragon
Bring dark sky, dragon
Oh, when will it come?

Try once again, dragon
Here comes the rain, dragon!
You have won, dragon
Dragon, well done!

Daniel Ellis-Fuller (8)
Berrynarbor Primary School, Ilfracombe

If Beds Had Wings

What if . . .
My bed grew wings
And I could fly away in my bed?
I would fly to Spain and Kenya
And Australia and Mars.
I would go to the beach in Spain
I would go to a house in Kenya
I would go to see the animals in Australia.
Is there a beach on Mars?

Sean Richardson (10)
Berrynarbor Primary School, Ilfracombe

Boneyard Rap

This is the rhythm
Of the Boneyard Rap
Tummies slap, teeth click
Click, clack, toes tinkle
All bones smack, whack
That's what happens
When you do
The Boneyard Rap whooooo
This is the rhythm
Of the Boneyard Rap
It's so good when you do
The rhythm of the Boneyard Rap.

Joseph Barnes (7)
Berrynarbor Primary School, Ilfracombe

Mother Nature

Mother Nature makes a flower
Each and every day
Mother Nature with her wand
Has the power to change the world
Mother Nature loves to work
Each and every day
She has a different expression
When the sky is black she's angry
When it rains she cries
But when it's sunny she's happy
And helps the flowers grow.

Simon Hopkins (8)
Berrynarbor Primary School, Ilfracombe

Mum

You're like a big, colourful rainbow,
A sun shining in light blue sky,
You're the ice cubes in a glass of limeade,
A happy tune coming from a piano,
You're like a gentle breeze on a summer's day,
Without you there would be no happiness.

Emma Hird (10)
Bickleigh-on-Exe Primary School, Bickleigh

TJ

You are the fuel in my mum's car
You are the back of the net when I whack the football
You are the Dr Pepper in my cup
You are the pencils in my pencil case
You are the pictures on my TV
You are the electronics in my PlayStation 2.

Alex Harwood (10)
Bickleigh-on-Exe Primary School, Bickleigh

Dad

You are the pepperoni on my pizza.
You're the warmth of my jumper when I get home from school.
You're the Dr Pepper slipping slowly down my throat.
You are a brilliant day out down the embankment.
You have my favourite colour blue on your jeans.
You help me train for football and get me into the football team.

Tom Justice (10)
Bickleigh-on-Exe Primary School, Bickleigh

The Mountain

The mountain towered in the distance
As the light crept down
The shadows grew
Soon the whole plain was dark
And the glass bottle on the picnic table vanished
As if it knew something we didn't.

A plane flew in to land
And the mountainous country beyond disappeared
Then the world filled with light
The glass bottle reappeared
And there were no longer any shadows.

Naomi Fuller (10)
Bickleigh-on-Exe Primary School, Bickleigh

Plane Crash

The light from the sun falls down,
As it hits the mountain,
Its shadow lands on the ground,
Debris from the plane crash still lying around,
Broken glass everywhere.

As the light fades,
The mountain gets smaller,
Now I can only just see the glass,
Moments before sunset I see the shadow of a man,
Crawling towards me.

Alice Rawlings (11)
Bickleigh-on-Exe Primary School, Bickleigh

Magic Mountain

As I climb to the top of the mountain the view looks so different
I see a horse galloping across the plain
I see glass shattering in an old rundown house
I see shadows from other buildings never seen before
The light up here is terrific, it's so warm and bright.

As I arrive at the bottom of the mountain
Everything's the right size again
I see the horse galloping across the plain in the distance
I see the remains of glass at my feet
Now I'm at the bottom of the mountain, the shadow creeps up on me
No longer is light burning so bright
Now an icy hand turns my blood cold.

Alicia Fotheringham (10)
Bickleigh-on-Exe Primary School, Bickleigh

The Glass Mountain

I looked at the glass mountain
It had no shadow and it was plain
There was just a mountain made of glass
With no shadow and it was plain
The light shone through it.

It started to cast a shadow
And it was plain no more
And the glass mountain started to glisten
The light shone through it.

Gareth Baker (11)
Bickleigh-on-Exe Primary School, Bickleigh

If The Owners Won't Bark

If the owners won't bark, the dogs will growl,
If the ghosts won't haunt, they'll probably howl.
If the children won't talk, their mouths will say,
If the parents won't hear, they've got their way.

If the people won't walk, their feet will start,
If the child won't pump blood, nor will the heart.
If the teacher won't scratch, chalk guaranteed will,
If the class has a headache, they'll take a pill.

If the people won't look, their eyes will stare,
If the man isn't bald, he'll have some hair.
If the world doesn't turn, half will be dark,
If the world has no water, there'll be no shark.

Saskia Loysen (10)
Bickleigh-on-Exe Primary School, Bickleigh

A Mountain Of Ice

A mountain of ice,
Its shadow a dark, gleaming fright,
With its colour of dirty glass,
It's plain to see that it is there,
Even in a dim light.

The heat of light cracks the ice,
With the sound of breaking glass,
As a plane flies over,
Its shadow looms closer,
Over that mountain of ice.

Bryoney Alford (9)
Bickleigh-on-Exe Primary School, Bickleigh

Today

The shadow is over,
Over the mountain.
No light in life,
Just darkness.

But light is on the horizon,
Where the white horse gallops across the plain,
To the mountain,
Where no one lives in the shadows,
Until the glass breaks.

Katie English (10)
Bickleigh-on-Exe Primary School, Bickleigh

My Best Friend

I have a best friend, she's good to me,
She's always there to look after me.
When I was a baby, she helped me to walk,
She even taught me how to talk.

She fed me in the day and night,
And comforted me when I had a fright.
She makes me laugh, she's very funny,
She even wipes my nose when runny.

She takes me out, we like to walk.
She's always there when I need to talk.
She cooks and cleans and irons my clothes,
And tidies my room, which she loathes.

When I don't behave as I should,
She tells me off and says, 'Gemma, be good."
My friend who is kind, good and fun,
Of course, you know now, she is *my mum*.

Gemma Cotter (9)
Bolham CP School, Tiverton

Cupid

Cupid flies up above
   And hits us with arrows of love
Even if the pairs are just not right
   He hits us when he's out of sight.

If you're bored, and you don't know what to do
   Then suddenly a boy comes running after you
Then he gives you a card and a bunch of flowers
   Then you really notice Cupid's special powers.

In Alaska, Canada, India, and England too
   What on earth are we going to do?
He's driving us mad, yes everyone around the world
   It's Cupid, with golden wings, and hair all curled.

But sometimes you get a different reaction
   When you notice someone nice in addition and subtraction
Then Cupid gets his arrows and fires away
   Then it turns out to be a really great day.

You go up to him, he comes up to you
   And then you know what you're going to do
You say hi, that's what you do
   He smiles and says that back to you.

Then you go over the top, and you hug and kiss
   Then somebody goes running, calling out, *'Miss!'*
A teacher comes out, calls you sexy cats!
   But you still got into trouble, and that is that.

But you don't care, and you still love each other
   Thanks, Cupid, for making us love one another
You're not that bad!
   This is the cutest love I ever had!

Bethany Lane (9)
Bolham CP School, Tiverton

There Once Was A Fairy

There once was a fairy who had a big fright
She never knew she had bad eyesight.

There once was a fairy whose name was Scary
She was utterly disgusting and very merry.

There once was a fairy who snored in her sleep
She bounced and she jumped, she even leaped.

There once was a fairy who had long hair
She made everyone stare but didn't really care.

There once was a fairy who had a big house
She would fly to the sky or ride on a mouse.

There once was a fairy who ate lots of fruit
She ran and she played, she even hid in a boot.

There once was a fairy who made little cakes
She would shout and whisper among the lakes.

There once was a fairy who played on a swing
She would laugh and giggle and even sing.

There once was a fairy who laid an egg
She would jump off a mountain and break her leg.

There once was a fairy who had a fat tummy
She begged and begged to her big mummy.

There once was a fairy who had big eyes
She told weird stories that were always lies.

There once was a fairy who said this is the end
Of this little poem.

Goodnight!

Sophie Hill (9)
Bolham CP School, Tiverton

My Dad

My dad is the best dad you could wish for
He buys me toys, he brings home sweets and chocolate
No dad is better than him
When I am sad he comes and makes me *happy* again
No dad is better than him
At night when I am cold
He comes and tucks me in
But best of all he is my dad
And I should not change him one tiny bit
And I am glad mummy married him.

Holly Drew (9)
Bolham CP School, Tiverton

The Tornado

I can come alive suddenly
And then disappear.

I can drag up anything
Even a child's tear.

Pulling up houses, trees and cars
Pulling restaurants, buses and bars.

You can hear the screaming
And see the glass gleaming as it stabs me, oh the pain.

Dragging up lives is like a million knives
Stabbing you slowly.

I am a tornado, not a nice flower
I cannot control myself . . .

But I do have power!

Ellen Howe (10)
Bolham CP School, Tiverton

My Dogs, Digglit and Russet

I have two dogs called Digglit and Russet,
I always thought them special.
The other night, without a ticket or permit,
They took a flit in a rocket.

By dressing up in an outfit,
(The helmet and jacket were not a tight fit)
And secretly sneaking aboard,
They climbed into the cockpit,
Fired up the circuits,
The rocket lit with a racket.

Nobody knew why,
The rocket roared into the sky.
A quick orbit round the moon,
Then they were home quite soon.
The reporters asked for their story,
I said, 'Excuse me, they'll only do it for money.'
They looked at me as if to say,
We wouldn't do it anyway!

Douglas Pullar (10)
Bolham CP School, Tiverton

Snow

I can cover the peak of a mountain, the fields of a farm
I can close the schools and block the doors
It's not my fault, it just happens
It's fun for the children and hard for the adults
I can fall whenever and make everyone cold
I can be a snowball or a snowman
And after everyone has played with me I start to cry
And then I disappear.

William Luxton (10)
Bolham CP School, Tiverton

Bad Little Piggy

Bad little piggy was baking a cake,
Baking a cake,
Baking a cake,
Bad little piggy was baking a cake,
Can you bake too?

Bad little piggy went walking along,
Walking along,
Walking along,
Bad little piggy went walking along,
Can you walk too?

Bad little piggy went visiting a friend,
Visiting a friend,
Visiting a friend,
Bad little piggy went visiting a friend,
Can you visit too?

Bad little piggy sat down to rest,
Sat down to rest,
Sat down to rest,
Bad little piggy sat down to rest,
Will you sit too?

Bad little piggy ate some cake,
Ate some cake,
Ate some cake,
Bad little piggy ate some cake,
Do you want some too?

Bad little piggy had no cake to give
No cake to give,
No cake to give,
Bad little piggy had no cake to give
Bad little piggy . . . and you!

Edward Pullar (7)
Bolham CP School, Tiverton

Crocodile

Here comes the *crocodile!*
Watch out, he's really vile!
If he comes to you
It's *snap! Crunch! Crack!*

Run for your life, here he comes!
Over the river,
Down to the house,
Quick, on the phone,
Call the animal control.
Hurry up! Hurry up!
Watch out, he's coming close,
Here's the control,
Quick, grab him,
He's too tough,
Let's raise the alarm,
Flee at once!

Michael Bevan (11)
Braunton Caen CP School, Braunton

Our Fire

Our fire crackles and burns,
It spits and hisses,
It warms us up on the coldest of days
To prepare us for the night.
When it dies down the embers glow
And they light the room at night.

Marcus Lywood (11)
Braunton Caen CP School, Braunton

My Cat Bagpuss!

My cat Bagpuss, so lazy, so fat,
My cat Bagpuss, the laziest cat!
He's hungry all night and he's hungry all day,
But when he's fed he's happy, hurray!
He's the king of our street,
He lies at our feet.
He sits by the fire, all cosy and warm,
But when he's angry he'll brew up a storm!
My cat Bagpuss, so lazy, so fat,
My cat Bagpuss, the laziest cat!

Aydan Greatrick (10)
Braunton Caen CP School, Braunton

Jungle Monkey

I'm in the jungle today, today,
Here's a monkey coming my way.
He's big and brown and jumping around,
Ran everywhere then fell to the ground.

I went over to him and said hello,
I'm sure he replied, 'Mento, mento.'
I heard him, I understood.
I do, I swear, I could, I could.
Maybe not my language
So it could be his,
I don't know.

Rachel Sandy (10)
Braunton Caen CP School, Braunton

Terrible Tiger

Strong, white striped tiger,
Running through the frost of the night.

Like a flash, he's out of sight,
Pouncing on his prey.
A little deer, there it lay,
All mangled in the light of the moon.

Night passes away,
The tiger lives to see another day.

Jasmine Whiteleaf (10)
Braunton Caen CP School, Braunton

The Sock Eater

The sock eater is a weird thing,
He chomps on socks, all kinds of sorts.
Smelly, dirty and wet too,
Even some which had a chew.
He makes a noise when he eats,
Sounds like your sister demanding treats.
It's horrible, I know,
It must go.
He once killed someone for a sock,
So it could be you next, tick-tock!

Jake Edwards (10)
Braunton Caen CP School, Braunton

How Does This Work?

'How does this work?'
'What work?'
'This work.'
'Oh, that work.
I don't know but I could never live without it!'

Rhiannon Jewell (10)
Braunton Caen CP School, Braunton

The Coldest Day

Today the ice age began,
The class radiators were broken,
And the ink inside our pens was frozen.
Our teacher suggested to watch TV,
Fifteen minutes passes slowly,
Hard to breathe, easy to sneeze.
The bell rang, children raced for freedom,
Never knowing what the next day would bring.

Hayley Swann (11)
Braunton Caen CP School, Braunton

Who Am I?

Who am I?
Where am I?
I can't see what's going on.
What's that noise?
Who's down there?
A tall person in front of me,
'Who's a cute little . . .'
What's a baby?

Victoria Pennington (11)
Braunton Caen CP School, Braunton

Have You Ever?

Have you ever heard a shark go woof?
Have you ever heard a dog go miaow?
Have you ever seen a pig fly in the sky
And sing Chow, Chow, Chow?
Have you ever heard a car go bang?
Have you ever heard a cannon go clang?
Have you ever?
Have you ever?
Have you ever?

Josh Murray (11)
Braunton Caen CP School, Braunton

My Hamster Minty

My hamster Minty, black and white,
Trying to escape in the darkest time of the night.
Chewing on the cage,
Now I'm full of rage.
But next morning the little devil's sound asleep.
I leave the room.
Suddenly a chewing noise came.
Oh no, he's at it again!
It became night once more, but no chewing.
I went to check,
He was dead.
Is it because he was overfed?
My hamster Minty is now dead.
Why couldn't it be the bird instead?

Kelly Swann (11)
Braunton Caen CP School, Braunton

Ice Cream

There's something delicious,
And it's called ice cream.
It comes in different flavours,
And tastes like a dream.
Strawberry, vanilla and chocolate too,
It's really, really sticky,
Just like pelican glue.

My favourite ice cream is a knickerbocker glory
Which is a totally different story!

Charlotte Hart (10)
Braunton Caen CP School, Braunton

The Rush To School

Beep, beep, beep, beep, beep
I'm late, I'm late!
Where's my socks?
Where's my jumper?
Boop, boop!
Oh no, it's the bus
I've missed my bus!
'Dad, Dad, where's my coat?'
Oh no, it's wet!
I haven't had my breakfast
'It's 10 to 9, Dad, I'm late!'
Dingalingaling, the school bell rings.
Lucky I woke up on time!

Izzy Brookes (10)
Braunton Caen CP School, Braunton

What Pig?

'Look at that pig in the sky!'
'What pig?'
'That pig, look at it fly.'
'I look, I see a flea!'
'Look at that flea climbing a tree!'
'What flea?'
'That flea, no larger than a pea.'
'There is no flea and no pig,
Your brain is no larger than a fig.'
'I was pulling your leg.'
'Me too, Peg.'
'You nit!'
'You're a twit!'

Libby Wastie (11)
Braunton Caen CP School, Braunton

Teachers!

Teachers get angry and they stink,
    When they get mad their faces go pink,
They bubble like stew,
    Should be flushed down the loo,
Then I won't need to think,
    I'll wash my knowledge down the sink!

Teachers always tell you what to do,
    It's funny how they never get the flu,
I want them gone
    What are they on?
You can see in their hair a slimy goo,
    Once in a while they start going moo!

Teachers hate me,
    Can't you see?
They step on your fingers, say accidentally,
    They don't care even if it's sore,
They just come back for more
    And more!

Detention they say
    And get more pay,
Excuses, excuses I throw in their face,
    I know you're good but I'm the ace!
You should have seen me in the middle of May,
    I threw a custard tart in her face, okay! Okay!

Jenny Coles (11)
Braunton Caen CP School, Braunton

I Love My Yorkshire Terriers

I love my Yorkshire Terriers,
They make me all the merrier,
They run as fast as a super jet,
I'm really glad they are my pets,
Their names are called Misty and Poppie,
Their ears are extremely floppy.

Liam Allman (10)
Braunton Caen CP School, Braunton

Splat!

Look at that bird, do you think it is rare?
Oh, do be careful.
Splat!
It's pooed in your hair.
Oh, I do look a mess.
So my friend she did sigh,
And then I was glad that cows couldn't fly.

Phoebe Reed (11)
Braunton Caen CP School, Braunton

Food 4 Parrot

There was once a little parrot
Who liked to eat a carrot
He also liked bananas
Which he stole from piranhas.

He was obsessed with food
But he was rather rude
He liked eating frozen chips
And getting ketchup on his lips.

He ate so much he got very fat
And fell off a tree into a cowpat
He tried to wash himself in a well
And then he heard the dinner bell.

He still rather smelt
And made the cheese melt
But he still ate his food
And was still excessively rude!

Sam Gardiner (10)
Coads Green Primary School, Launceston

The A-Z Of The African Bush

A nnoying aardvarks were eating the ants,
B ouncing baboons made the noise,
C hasing cheetahs are the predators,
D azzling dassies look so sweet upon a rock,
E xtraordinary elephants sprayed the water,
F loundering flamingos are easy to sight,
G orgeous giraffes use their metre-long necks,
H yper hippos roam the waters,
I diotic impalas glide through the sky,
J umping jackals hunting in the night,
K icking kudu have glistening eyes,
L aughing leopards leap from ground to tree,
M unching mongooses looking for insects,
N aughty nyalas look through the savannah,
O ccupied ostriches carry on trying to fly,
P eacemaking pangolins rolling into balls,
Q ueen quails glide up high,
R aging rhinos start a charge,
S lithering snakes hissing and spitting,
T alking tortoises come to you slowly,
U nsighted, unstoppable animals which are hardly seen,
V ipers, vicious creatures crawling along,
W alking warthogs rolling around in the mud,
X treme, extraordinary birds fly through the clouds,
Y awning yellow birds which are unable to fly,
Z imbabwean zebras completes the African Bush.

Sammy Wheeler (10)
Coads Green Primary School, Launceston

The Silver-Coloured Moon

T he moon shines silver as the stars start to dazzle,
H urrying across the star-filled sky goes a cloud
                                    that looks like a horse.
E veryone looks up to see the cloud that goes running
                                    upon the lumpy moon.

S now starts to fall as it gets really cold,
I ce starts to show over some disgusting green mould.
L ight starts to fail of the brightly-coloured moon,
V enus can be seen so very far away.
E ager to fade the cloud it goes,
R acing the shooting stars to the moon.

M unching on the planet Saturn rainbow rings,
O n the moon someone starts to sing.
O nce every night the cloud horse comes out,
'N ight is here,' the cloud person shouts.

Rosanna Dinnis (10)
Coads Green Primary School, Launceston

The Little Welsh Cob

Galloping, galloping across the sand
Swishing his tail as much as he can
The little Welsh cob roaming the land.

Cantering, cantering as fast as he can
His mane shining in the summer's sun
The little Welsh cob has ran.

Trotting, trotting to his Welsh mum
Stopped to have a lie down
The little Welsh cob is having fun.

Walking, walking when the sky turns brown
Turns to his mum desperate to stop
The little Welsh cob has to lie down.

Elizabeth Hosking (9)
Coads Green Primary School, Launceston

Quick!

Quick, quick!
Get out
There's a fire about
Run for your lives
Get your wives
The babies cry
They might die.

Quick, quick!
Get out
There's a fire about
Call the fire brigade
The building is starting to fade
Nee Nor, Nee Nor, Nee Nor
Here comes the fire brigade.

Quick, quick!
Get out
Now it's gone
The bells go ding-dong
It gave up a fight
In the middle of the night
Yeah! It's gone!

Ben Berger (11)
Coads Green Primary School, Launceston

Nothingness

Icy cold.
No feelings.
Blank.
Plain.
Nothing exists.
Nothing there.
Inspirationless.
Nothingness.
Bleakly silent.
Frozen still.
Bare.
Bleached,
Whitely cold.
No sound.
Doesn't exist.
Nothingness.
Shivery still.
Can't be there.
Just ice.
Non existent.
All alone.
Strangely still.
Gone forever.
Nothingness.

Carly Halls (10)
Coads Green Primary School, Launceston

Flowers

Daffodils are yellow and bright,
Roses are quite a sight.

Daisies are white and light,
Sunflowers grow quite a height.

Tulips are green and red,
Poppies grow in flower beds.

Bluebells grow in the summer,
Pansies are much duller.

Snowdrops fall to the ground,
Carnations are never found.

Honeysuckle smell very sweet,
Primroses don't like the heat.

All these flowers I would send,
And now this is the end.

Jordan James (10)
Coads Green Primary School, Launceston

Horses

Across the fresh cut, grassy hill,
The horses run at their own free will,
Their clean, black coats shine in the sun,
They're looking out to have some fun.

Their dark black manes blowing as they trot,
Jumping over logs that have started to rot,
Trotting through a cold river,
Which did make them quiver.

After their adventure this night,
The moon came out to shine its light,
After this the horses went home,
The hills and moors are never alone.

Ben Norgate (11)
Coads Green Primary School, Launceston

The Black Stallion

I gallop across the moonlit beach,
My hooves sinking in the wet sand,
I am the black stallion who's always been here,
Roaming all over the land, animals obeying my command.

I turn and slow down,
And canter off into the sea,
In this quiet little cove,
It's only the white horses and me, people know I'm here but they
let me be.

I bolt out of the sea,
I turn and up the cliff path I go,
Here it is winter with a storm in action,
The icy wind makes my mane blow, as I thunder across
the glittering snow.

I now am in a wood, with animals bowing at my presence,
It is spring with animals and plants all around,
There are animals and rodents running here and there,
Their feet pit-pattering across the ground, making a pleasant sound.

I am in a grassy field, summertime is here,
A golden sun is hanging in a bright blue sky,
Bees are buzzing around the old withered trees,
As I canter round I wonder why, how birds can but I can't fly.

I trot through a wood but it is autumn this time,
Leaves cover the ground like a carpet of yellow, red, brown and gold,
I would love to stay here but I must go now,
I return to my beach as the evening becomes old, the moon shines
bright and bold.

I gallop across the moonlit beach,
My hooves sinking in the wet sand,
I am the black stallion who's always been here,
Roaming all over the land, animals obeying my command.

I stay here on my own with the white horses and the sea,
People know I am here but they let me be,
It is just the sea and me.

Isabel Brumwell (10)
Coads Green Primary School, Launceston

Tiger

Watch out, the tiger's about
Killing, stalking, pouncing
He's out at night, the prey's in the corner
It can't get out, the tiger pounces
Gives the prey a fright.

The tiger misses, the prey runs out
The tiger follows but sees a deer
The deer's thinking *what's that about?*
The tiger, the deer can't hear.

The tiger's low, starting to stalk
It steps closer to its prey
The birds squawk
The birds move away.

The tiger pounces for his prey
This time there is no miss
Dead on the floor the prey lays
As the tiger hisses.

James Goodman (9)
Coads Green Primary School, Launceston

Summer Sun

The summer looked, its burning, blazing, furious glare,
A stare so bright and warm, that held inside an inner storm.

It took itself high into the sky, like a bright golden king
                                                    of the summertime.
It lifted itself to the top of Rame Head,
A burning, blazing ball of red.

Up it went into the clouds and as if it said aloud,
'I'm going to go and I will not stay
So I hope that you know there is going to be a cold, cold snow.'

Ralph Arscott (10)
Fourlanesend CP School, Torpoint

Cornwall Is The Place To Be

Cornwall is the place to be
All summer long, feeling happy and free!
The bumpy hills blend with Millbrook,
The tiny daisies dotting the fanciful fields,
The scrummy smells of sweetness flying up my nose,
The rustling sounds of the trees,
Fluffy clouds covering up the clear blue sky,
The painful sounds of seagulls twirping,
The white horses crash against the ragged rocks of Kingsand,
The slight smell of the fishy seas.

Cornwall is the place to be
All summer long, feeling happy and free!

Maizey Peters (11)
Fourlanesend CP School, Torpoint

Summer Has Come To Cornwall

Summer has come to Cornwall,
Shining on Rame Head church.

Summer has come to Cornwall,
People in the sea.

Summer has come to Cornwall,
People having BBQs.

Summer has come to Cornwall,
People having ice creams.

Summer has come to Cornwall,
People jumping off Pimper.

Summer has come to Cornwall,
Shining in just one place
That place is Rame Peninsula.

Joshua Willcocks (11)
Fourlanesend CP School, Torpoint

Surfer's Barbie On The Beach

Everyone in Cornwall is enjoying the sun,
Sandwiches out of seagull's reach,
Now is the time to tell everyone,
There's a surfer's barbie on the beach!

Down in Cawsand is the place to be,
Careful of the seagull's screech,
I smell sausages made for me,
At the surfer's barbie on the beach!

When you're in the mood,
Or when boring old priests start to preach,
You know just what to do,
Head to the surfer's barbie on the beach!

Get down there and surf your best,
Take a board each,
You don't need to be a guest,
To join the surfer's barbie on the beach!

Tom Kendall (11)
Fourlanesend CP School, Torpoint

The Sun Of The Forgotten Corner

The summer sun is burning the beach
But far away in Edgcombe grows the nutritious peach.
On the beach of Whitsand the surf is clean
So the famous surfers of Whitsand will be riding mean.

While elders lie on . . .
Catching the glorious sun.
Phil is doing fine with those chips so divine.

Here in Cornwall is the place to be,
With the summer sun and the transparent sea.

Thomas Calladine (11)
Fourlanesend CP School, Torpoint

The Summer Fairies!

The summer fairies come to play,
The summer fairies play all day.
They touch the cold and make it warm,
Which helps the flowers to grow and form.

They travelled from Cawsand to Rame,
Then they flew along the coast to Whitsand Bay.
Then they flew on to Looe and bought a fish or two!
They then flew to Polperro and sat on the beach for a while:
Half an hour after, they were back in their dens . . . hiding!

Lisa Marie Baker (11)
Fourlanesend CP School, Torpoint

A Cornish Summer

Sweet smells of freshly cut grass and flowers,
Children playing on golden, sandy beaches hour after hour.
Hill upon hill of gently swaying trees,
The occasional hum of honey-making bees.
The calm lapping of the sea against the boat,
The still shimmer of the mirror which keeps it afloat.
Salty chips and sticky ice cream,
Swinging in a hammock in a daydream.

Bonnie Farley (11)
Fourlanesend CP School, Torpoint

Happiness

I can see the view over the horizon
I can hear the birds sing
and the trees glisten.
I can see the cows eat the grass
I can see the field and the buildings far away
I can hear the breeze
I can hear the children talking, smiling
and playing with each other.

Darren Mitchell (10)
Fourlanesend CP School, Torpoint

A Cornish Summer

A Cornish summer
has green all around
and swaying, rustling leaves sound.

A Cornish summer
has turquoise sea running
through your feet
and that gentle breeze.

A Cornish summer
has a lovely breeze
through your hair
and waves lapping of joy everywhere.

Is that a Cornish summer?

Chloe Adams (10)
Fourlanesend CP School, Torpoint

Summer

The cool water beckons all to come,
The flaming sun burns all unaware,
As Tom jumps into the paddling pool
And splashes Luke and Will,
Whilst children do play on the beach.

While Frank does a perfect barrel ride,
All let out a gasp,
The sparkling sea welcomes all,
The summer grass dazzles the eye,
And the daisies sway in the breeze,
Whilst children do play on the beach.

Everybody helps Tom with the BBQ,
Yet for others, time for fun.

Of course it's summer!

Sam Wacher-Carne (10)
Fourlanesend CP School, Torpoint

Summer Is Here

Summer is here, summer is here,
The sky is bright, the sky is clear,
The birds and sea is all I hear,
Summer is here, summer is here.

Summer is here, summer is here,
I'd love to go outside and smell
The wonderful trees casting spells,
Summer is here, summer is here.

Summer is here, summer is here,
There are moths, butterflies and bees,
And larvaes making cocoons in the trees,
Summer is here, summer is here.

Summer is here, summer is here,
I love to see the Rame church,
Whilst birds on trees perch,
Summer is here, summer is here.

Lillian Rogers (9)
Fourlanesend CP School, Torpoint

The Summer Of Cornwall!

Is it the sun that makes me shine,
or is it just me?
Is it the breeze that makes me feel cheerful,
or is it just me?
The breeze of the air,
the shine of the sun,
yes, it's the summer of Cornwall!

Is it the grass that makes me feel fresh,
or is it just me?
Is it the sea that makes me wonder,
or is it just me?
The freshness of the grass,
the wonders of the sea,
yes, it's the summer of Cornwall!

Emma Platts (10)
Fourlanesend CP School, Torpoint

Lost Cornish Summer

The sun is beating down,
The Cornish hills are green.
The people turning brown,
The jackdaw being mean.

The surf is curling up the sand,
The Cornish hills are green.
The water trickles through my hand,
The trees begin to lean.

No one knows where Cawsand is,
It's like it was never there.
Every time it's always missed,
You'll never find his lair.

Ryan Cooper (11)
Fourlanesend CP School, Torpoint

The Three Witches

Double, double toil and trouble;
Fire burn and cauldron bubble,
Snippet of a dog's bladder,
Splinter of a human ladder,
Eye of a huge shark,
The ring of a small bark,
A hag's frightful laugh,
A piece of pizza in half,
Double, double toil and trouble;
Fire burn and cauldron bubble.

Josh Pike (10)
Hayward CP School, Crediton

Universe

U nknown planets waiting to be discovered,
N earby a slither of moon deepening,
I n deep space lies a hole of darkness,
V enus, the gas giant, not to harm but to seek,
E arth spinning, tilting, twisting,
R eflecting eclipse like a sparkling sheet of silver,
S un, the energy of our meaningful lives,
E quator, the rotating depth.

Esther Thorn Gent (10)
Hayward CP School, Crediton

Suffering Deserts

Infinite sand dunes standing firm
Stinging scorpions here and there
Sticky, scorching heat blazing in the suffering sky
Slithering snakes wriggle across the patterned sand
Flat mountains of dusty sand.

Ben Reed (9)
Hayward CP School, Crediton

Dogs

Cat-chaser
Ball-fetcher
People-player
Bed-sleeper
River-splasher
Grass-digger
Ball-fetcher
Flea-biter
Mean-prowler.

Natalie Armstrong (10)
Hayward CP School, Crediton

Cat

Basket-defender
Ground-padder
Fur-archer
Paw-pusher
Dog-fighter
Rabbit-stalker
Rug-stretcher
Fish-pouncer
Fly-biter
Bird-chaser
Fence-leaper
Tree-grabber.

Jessica Bailey (9)
Hayward CP School, Crediton

Monkey

Cheeky-smiler
Excited-jumper
Tree-climber
Fruit-muncher
Fun-player
Branch-swinger.

Amy Hill (9)
Hayward CP School, Crediton

Universe

Jupiter-spinner
Asteroid-orbiter
Meteor-showerer
Milky Way-explorer
Universe-masterer
Earth-ozone layer.

Aaron Davey (10)
Hayward CP School, Crediton

The Three Hags

Double, double toil and trouble,
Fire burn and cauldron bubble.

Slime of snail,
Fin of whale,
Eyelid of frog,
Black of fog,
Fang of bat,
One-eyed cat,
Black worm's bladder,
A spell to make it madder,
For a charm of powerful trouble,
Like a Hell broth boil and bubble.

Double, double toil and trouble,
Fire burn and cauldron bubble.

Michelle Soper (10)
Hayward CP School, Crediton

Three Witches

Double, double toil and trouble
Fire burn and cauldron bubble
A short hair of a bat
A furry tail of a tabby cat
A long, red tongue of a frog
A nose of a muddy hog
A feather of a colourful bird
A tusk from each elephant herd
A squeak from a deadly rat
A fierce brown dog on a mat
Double, double toil and trouble
Fire burn and cauldron bubble.

Charlotte Parsons (10)
Hayward CP School, Crediton

Solar System

Earth-revolver
Mars-freezer
Sun-exploder
Pluto-spinner
Jupiter-stormer
Saturn-ringer
Uranus-gasser
Asteroid-floater
Meteor-flyer.

Owaen Guppy (10)
Hayward CP School, Crediton

Space

Moon-dancer
Astronaut-zoomer
Planet-orbiter
Sun-burner
Rocket-lander
Earth-spinner
Star-twister.

Liam Lowey (10)
Hayward CP School, Crediton

Olympics

60 metre-sprinter
High-jumper
Long-thrower
Loud-commentator
Gun-shooter
Marathon-jogger
Water-splasher
Triple-leaper.

Lewis Pinn (10)
Hayward CP School, Crediton

The Highwayman

(Based on 'The Highwayman' by Alfred Noyes)

The sunrise was a blazing ball of fire among the bony trees,
The dancing leaves were a scattered ship on an ocean breeze,
The road was covered in darkness spreading over the moor,
The highwayman came driving -
Driving, driving
The highwayman came driving up to the old, crooked stable door.

He wore a baseball cap on his head,
His trousers black and thin as a pencil lead,
Black leather boots that reached his thigh,
He drove with a jewelled twinkle,
A sparkling twinkle,
The sun was warming in the midday sky.

Over the bridge he drove so fast,
Parking outside the stable at last,
He knocked on the door and who is standing there,
But the stable man's youngest daughter,
Kasy, the stable man's daughter,
Plaiting a pony tail in her long, blonde hair.

Stephanie Yelland (9)
Hayward CP School, Crediton

The Three Witches

Double, double toil and trouble,
Fire burn and cauldron bubble.
A whipping tail of a snake,
The tip of a still lake,
A tooth of a mole,
A toad or frog roll,
An eye of a bat,
The tail of a cat,
A hair of a wizard,
A watery blizzard,
Double, double toil and trouble,
Fire burn and cauldron bubble.

Sean Mills (9)
Hayward CP School, Crediton

Fun Football

Shot-saver
Long-passer
Good-tackler
Hard-shooter
Goal-scorer
Mud-mover
Quick-sprinter
Excited-player
Free kick-taker.

Daniel Boddy (10)
Hayward CP School, Crediton

In Space

Meteor-stormer
Universe-grower
Milky Way-spinner
Sun-eclipser
Galaxy-swirler
Jupiter-surrounder
Spacecraft-zoomer
Asteroid-floater
Earth-orbiter
Gravity-holder.

Michael Raymont (10)
Hayward CP School, Crediton

Space

Mercury-mover
Earth-rumbler
Venus-erupter
Mars-revolver
Sun-burner.

Brecon Eveleigh (10)
Hayward CP School, Crediton

The Highwayman

(Based on 'The Highwayman' by Alfred Noyes)

The sunrise was an explosion of fire among the ghostly trees,
The darkness had gone but made a light breeze,
The road was an icy streak of glass across the misty moor,
The highwayman came driving,
Driving, driving,
The highwayman came driving up to the Mafia door.

He had a cap with a New York logo and a barbed wire tattoo
round his neck,
He had a black, sleeveless hoody and a 500 Euro cheque,
His jeans and Adidas trainers showed him as a gangster, you'll see,
His shotgun in his pocket,
Hid deep beneath his pocket,
50 bullets on guard like a referee.

Over the road he skidded and screeched,
To the headquarters of the Mafia he reached.
He said the password and who should be waiting there,
But the Godfather chief Mafia,
Alexendo, the chief Mafia,
Styling a quiff in dark black hair.

Fred Conyngham (9)
Hayward CP School, Crediton

Stars

S tretch of black velvet covers the sky,
T he solar system reaches far and wide.
A re there any more life forms way up in the darkness?
R ide on the stars and see for yourself,
S un is our saviour, our ruler, we can't live without it . . .

Lisa Chart (10)
Hayward CP School, Crediton

Space

N ever-ending space,
E xploring stars around the galaxy,
U p in space where there is no gravity,
T he dead still planets orbiting around the sun,
R ound the solar system in a spacecraft
O rbiting the Earth, where will the spacecraft go?
N uclear reaction releases a vast amount of energy.

S upernova! A bright, new star,
T earing, twisting solar system,
A universe full of stars and planets,
R ed giant in utter stillness.

Kaylee Branch (9)
Hayward CP School, Crediton

The Storm

The storm is noisy,
the storm is loud,
the storm is dangerous,
the storm is found.

The storm is crashing,
the storm is smashing,
the storm is bashing,
and electrically flashing.

The storm is thundering,
the storm is rumbling,
I don't like storms,
so now I'm trembling.

Arthur Sayers (11)
Honiton CP School, Honiton

My Feelings

I feel down sometimes
when people shout at me
because I got something wrong
or I am very naughty.

I feel happy most times
when people are friendly
because I've done something
to help them mostly.

I feel scared sometimes
when I am alone in my bed
wind blowing roughly
I wake up with a bad head.

I feel excited sometimes
when I am going on a trip
or I am at work
and my boss gives me a tip.

But when I feel angry
my fist curls like a ball
then I think of getting told off
I don't hit anyone at all.

Daniel Cooke (10)
Honiton CP School, Honiton

Fireworks!

We're going to see the fireworks
up high in the sky.
All the pretty colours,
makes you want to cry.

Pink, green, yellow,
red, gold, blue.
Not only that
there are effective sounds too!

All the intricate patterns
like stars and swirls.
No straight lines,
all of them are curls.

The fire's still burning,
plenty more to come.
My eyes can't stop staring,
it's so much fun.

Now it's nearly over,
everyone's going home.
I'm staying for the last of them,
and going home alone.

Danielle Gillard (11)
Honiton CP School, Honiton

Cats

Meowwww
Cries the cat
Scratching and clawing
Loops from the sofa
Can make it annoying.

Purrrr
Cries the cat
Its purr is soft
And comforting
It puts you in a trance
Makes you follow to the loft.

Meowwww
Cries the cat
In a fearsome battle
Arching his back
And it suddenly spat.

Purrrr
Cries the cat
All soft and comforting
Its purr is secret
Just for you
The purr will always be with you
Never crinkling.

Meowwww
Cries the cat
Returning from adventure
Until another day
Until another venture.

Samuel Bath (10)
Honiton CP School, Honiton

My Magic Fingers And Hat

My funny, flapping fingers,
Tingle like my toes,
My hairy, hunched hat,
Covers up my nose.

They flap like wings,
To make my wishes,
It doesn't help me,
When it comes to dishes.

It comes to life,
While I sleep,
It's like it doesn't,
Make a peep.

It's a horrible time,
When it comes to awaking,
When my mum,
Expects me to do the baking.

I'm frying the lunch just before the break,
If I want lunch,
I'll have to make
A wish with my magic fingers and hat.

Kelly Kennard (11)
Honiton CP School, Honiton

The Football Match

The crowds are on their feet,
They are chanting as loud as a herd of elephants,
The sound of studs hitting the ground,
Travelling through the tunnel.
The spectators roar as the players enter.

Excitement fills the air
Ready for the game to begin,
The whistle goes and the crowd chant, 'More!'
Red card held up high,
Player walking out with head hung low.

Tension rising when player approaching the goal,
Player strikes the ball into the back of the net,
Spectators are on their feet chanting, '1-0,'
Opposite supporters are booing.

Matthew Dunn (10)
Honiton CP School, Honiton

Different Colours

I paint bright colours when I am happy
But when I am unhappy or sad
I look into the air with sadness
And think of black and grey
Which soon makes me think
Of how lucky I really am.

Red speaks to me with the beauty of a poppy.
Yellow reminds me of the sun
And the sandy plains of the desert
But green is my favourite colour.
It is not sad or happy
It is only plain.

Lawrence Lane (11)
Honiton CP School, Honiton

Imagine

Imagine you flew in a plane
across the blue sky.
Imagine your engine exploded,
that's when you really fly.

Imagine you sailed all 7 seas,
in a little wooden boat.
The tide is so rough,
it's hard to stay afloat.

Imagine your mind
wild and free.
Imagine you climbed
the highest tree.

The tree terribly torn,
it killed your hand so much
that when you fall
you fall to the sand.

Imagine careless ages
passing beneath your feet.
Imagine the world growing hungry
because there is nothing to eat.

Jorden S Treacey (11)
Honiton CP School, Honiton

Labrador

L ively, loving Labradors
A lways having fun
B othering people at parks playing
R ough with their dogs getting
A ttention from other people who
D oze off to sleep
O r even make a
R acket by shouting at other dogs.

Emma Kingston (11)
Honiton CP School, Honiton

My Four Fab Friends

There are five of us altogether
me and my four fab friends
I'm the oldest
but that doesn't matter
because our friendship
will never end.

Of course we have rows
nearly every couple of weeks
well, just about silly things
like who's next to speak.

We stick together
like paper and glue
always thinking
of something to do.

We never feel sad
when either one of us is around
we have a laugh
we hang around.

We do everything together
having sleepovers
and chilling out
we'll always be friends
forever and ever.

Tayseer Elmaghdy (11)
Honiton CP School, Honiton

My Dog

My dog Milly,
Is so precious,
She loves us, we thank her
She eats like a lion,
She sniffs like a hog,
But she never forgets,
She is family!

She runs free like a horse,
And glides like a hawk,
And when she runs,
She passes through into her own world!

When she goes to the forest all you see
Is a white blur,
She bawls like a hair hound,
And eats like a pig,
And acts like a puppy
But is not!

She runs free like a cheetah,
And as fast as a greyhound,
And as strong as a rhino,
And a personality like her dad,
My dad,
And she always remembers
She's family.

George Meadows (11)
Honiton CP School, Honiton

Crazy Cricket Crowd

Crazy cricket crowd
Cheer the champions as
England ease into victory
The World Cup was theirs.

The crowd go wild
England ecstatic as
The crazy crowd
Invade the pitch.

The coloured jerseys of the England team
Have turned green
The ground's empty seats
Look so bare.

Everyone is on the pitch
Except the West Indies fans
Now it's time for the man of the match
Who will it be?

Martyn Schmidt (11)
Honiton CP School, Honiton

Different

They say I'm a geek,
Girls say I look like a freak.
Each time I go to school,
It's like I'm from out of space.
They look at me like I'm a piece of rubbish,
They say I'm disabled -
The teachers just glare
But what do I care?
I look in the mirror,
But all I see is me -
Sad and friendless.
It's not my fault,
I'm just different.

Donovan Spencer (10)
Honiton CP School, Honiton

The Hunt

The panther's sleek black coat shone in the sun's light,
He was silently stalking a deer,
He hid in the long, green grass out of everyone's sight,
Ready to strike at any moment.

His green eyes focused on his prey,
He was determined to catch something to eat,
For he was hungry every day,
Was he in for a treat today?

He knew he only had one chance, it was now or never,
He moved in for the kill,
The scorching hot weather,
Reduced the deer's reaction.

In no time at all,
He had caught the deer,
For it was only small,
The best meal in weeks.

Jennifer Hole (11)
Honiton CP School, Honiton

My Sister

My sister can be annoying sometimes
My sister can be selfish sometimes
My sister can be horrible sometimes
My sister gets me told off sometimes
Me and my sister fall out sometimes

But I love my sister sometimes
Because she's funny sometimes
She does stuff for me sometimes
She lets me play with her friends sometimes
She gets me stuff sometimes
She's good at sport sometimes.

Alexander Sandason (11)
Honiton CP School, Honiton

My Brothers

They are annoying
They dob
It is like their job
They keep me awake especially Jake
They break my toys
Then run away
Call me names
Rip paper off my birthday presents
They think it will help!

Jake is fussy
Ashley sucks his thumb
They break my toys
I say, 'I'll tell mum.'
There are good things as well
We watch TV together
Play football with each other
And I am glad they are not sisters!

Bradley Ablett (11)
Honiton CP School, Honiton

Secret Agents

Secret agents running around town
Secret agents swimming through seas
Secret agents hiding from villains
Secret agents swerving through doors
Secret agents slip away
Secret agents escaping
Secret agents going back to base
Secret agents stealing designs
Secret agents gathering secrets
Secret agents going through doors
Secret agents going off duty
Secret agents going to bed.

Jamie Lynn (10)
Honiton CP School, Honiton

Fish

Fish are colourful
Fish are grey
Fish are black
Some are prey.

Fish are fat
Fish are small
Fish are slimy
Some are cool.

Fish look dopey
Fish look sad
Fish look happy
Fish look glad.

Fish have eyes
Fish have tails
Fish have gills
Some have scales.

Fish all eat
Fish all drink
Fish all sleep
Fish can't think.

Terence Rich (11)
Honiton CP School, Honiton

The Full Moon

The full moon is like a ping-pong ball bouncing around.
The full moon is like an eye spying down.
The full moon is gazing and shining down.
The full moon's creamy sparkle giving us light.

Ryan Dunn (7)
Honiton CP School, Honiton

Young Writers - Once Upon A Rhyme Devon & Cornwall   63

The Writer Of This Poem

(Based on 'The Writer Of This Poem' by Roger McGough)

The writer of this poem is . . .

She has lots of colourful locks,
As smelly as old socks,
As square as a box,
Smarter than a teacher,
Slyer than a fox,
As dead as a dodo,
As strong as an ox,
As tall as a tree,
As royal as the Queen,
As fierce as a lion,
As sweet as sugar,
As stiff as cardboard,
As tired as a koala,
As cuddly as a cat,
As fussy as my sister,
As hungry as a hippo,
As funny as a clown,
As light as a feather,
As colourful as the rainbow,
As sexy as a super model.

That's me!

Rozie-Erin Bentley (11)
Honiton CP School, Honiton

Forever Friends

I love my friends,
They're the best,
In all the west,
I can tell them everything, I know.

My best friend is Hanz
She's the best,
She is so special to me 'cause,
She listens to my problems.

Shanz is such a diva girl,
She's the best,
Shanz is so cool to play with,
But very annoying.

Nazi is such a girly girl,
She's the best,
She makes me laugh,
She's very good at lying, I wish I was her.

Tay is a very funky girl,
She's the best,
She has a great sense of fashion,
That's what I like about Tay.

It doesn't matter what order I put them in,
'Cause,
They are all the bestest friends,
In all the world.

Melodie Blake (11)
Honiton CP School, Honiton

Nagging Parents

Please do this
Please do that
Please may you
Groom the cat.

Don't do this
Don't do that
Don't you dare
Walk into the flat.

Go up Tesco
Do the drying
I really think
You're frying.

Don't you think
You're the crown
Just as you're
In the town?

While you're out
Please behave
I don't want you
To be in a grave.

We're going out
Out with the family
You're going to have dinner
So I expect you to be the winner.

Surely though
You'll be smart
But then again
You're very good at art.

So now you've heard
My nagging parents
So bear in mind
That you'll always be nagged.

Jenty Flynn (11)
Honiton CP School, Honiton

Lulu

Miaowing loudly
Purring for her food
Playing with her kittens
She's in a happy mood.

Cat sat on the rug
Purring peacefully on the mat
She's trying to sleep
In her dreams she keeps chasing rats.

The cat pounced
For the string
She always does this
Silly thing.

Sharpens her claws
Digs through the ground
She's trying to catch birds
She's not making a sound.

Cat yawning
Forgetting her prey
She thinks she will sleep
For a whole day.

Jessica Wakley (10)
Honiton CP School, Honiton

The Gale

The wind howls through the bending streets
Singing as it goes.
Flying, spiralling and finally dying down.

The moon appears in the gale
Like a flying saucer.
The moon swirls in the glistening night sky.
The wind pushes up the lane.
Flying cars go down your street.
Off it goes again.

As lightning crashes
The slates fall off rooftops.
Finally it settles down
It disappears through the town.

Nathan Mugford (10)
Honiton CP School, Honiton

The Elephant Story

It's long, scaly trunk is just like a snake,
Its short, thin eyelashes, just like two rakes.
But do we stop to think what it might do?
Do we ever stop to think
That it doesn't belong in a zoo?

Elephants are killed and slaughtered
For their long, ivory tusks.
Elephants are killed and slaughtered
From dawn until dusk.
Why don't hunters stop and think?
What have they ever done to us?

Abigail Webber (10)
Honiton CP School, Honiton

Silent Assassin

He moves swiftly,
But lightly,
In the shadows,
He kills if he must,
In the dark,
Is invisible,
Amazing,
Like a leech on a beast,
Never letting go.

A dangerous mission,
His heart thuds,
He is not nervous,
When he kills,
When he hangs,
From a pipe,
Just tries not,
To breathe loudly,
When he is done,
He is gone.

Alexander Thornton (10)
Honiton CP School, Honiton

Werewolves

Werewolves reek of flesh
And dried up blood
They're blood-thirsty
They just wait for you to go past
They eat your flesh
They crunch your bones
Their eyes are
Deep and hungry-looking.

Harry Stoneman (11)
Honiton CP School, Honiton

Fantastic Gymnastic!

I really do love gym
It makes me wanna smile
It's better than everything
Even running a whole mile!

I have a lovely-looking leotard
It's really, really bright
We are good, gorgeous gymnasts
We think of winning every night!

I love to laugh and joke
It's not ever a bad place
Who would want to leave?
It's like my own base!

We perform when we're told
We agree with our friends
People say I'm flexible
And my back really bends!

It's a really exciting club
I always want to go
If mum says let's go to the gym
I'll never say *no!*

I'm a fantastic gymnast!

Kia Mortimer-Wale (11)
Honiton CP School, Honiton

Choco Day

Chocolate is my favourite thing
It is lovely, delicious
I wait till I get home
I eat it in a cone.

My mum thinks I'm really mad
Because I love chocolate really bad
And when I haven't got it
I feel really sad.

I should have been called Chocolate
'Cos chocolate is my thing
When I have chocolate
It makes me want to sing.

I give my cat some chocolate
Whenever I am bored
Even though I am not supposed to
But I swing it on a cord.

When I die
I will take some chocolate
With me in a pie
So I won't cry.

Leanne Butcher (11)
Honiton CP School, Honiton

The Hill

Another hill coming up
But we haven't gone down the last one yet
Getting into first gear to go up it
Here we go. Go, go, go, pedal, pedal, pedal.

Up the hardest of the lot
'Stop at the top,' says my dad
I'll be happy to
Eventually, here it comes, the top
Brakes on, feet down.

Here we are, get over the fence
Wow, we're in a downhill forest
Bump, bump, bump down the hill we go
Here comes a root
Wheee, that was fun
Hey, a turning
The path stops, better turn
Oh no, it's the end!

Daniel Bewsey (11)
Honiton CP School, Honiton

Hurricanes

Destroyer
Fast destroyer
Destroying everything in its path
Smashing things as we speak.

Cracking slates off rooftops
Thrashing treetops
The winds blow at speed
Smashing houses right down to the floor
Like a flower pulled out of the ground.

Lee Clark (11)
Honiton CP School, Honiton

Fairy-Tale Forest

Dark and gloomy fairy-tale forest,
Tall trees swaying in the breeze,
Weird witches, eerie elves,
Frivolous fairies, irksome imps.
Toadstools, mushrooms begin to grow,
A starless fairy-tale forest in the night-time mist.
Creepy sounds as you walk in,
But as you get in deeper,
Towards the heart of the forest,
You hear ghostly sounds,
Deadlier than the echo of the owl,
In the midnight wind.
The screech of the bat,
The rustle of the leaves in the wind,
The forest is a frightening place at night,
Dark and spooky.

Suzette Blackmore (11)
Honiton CP School, Honiton

The Moon!

The moon is looking down on me
Spying like a German spy.
A giant golf ball like a headlight
Getting torched by the sun.

The moon is like a silvery white bottle top
Screwing on a bottle high up in space

The moon is like a clock
Moving its hands
Minute by minute.

Arthur Palmer York (8)
Honiton CP School, Honiton

Killing The World

Thick, black paste,
Killing creatures,
Making toxic waste,
Discolouring all the features,
Washed up on the shore,
Black, black sea will never be colourful again,
What have they done to be ignored?
Sea creatures now we always see in pain.

Plastic beer holders trapping fish,
Drowning dolphins,
People won't have as many fish dishes,
People not frowning,
Fish dying, we're not crying,
People see yet they don't care,
No more fish flying,
We're more interested in our hair.

Whales, they've done nothing wrong,
People just want red lips,
Now we will never hear their song,
We throw them out like pips.

Alex Chambers (11)
Honiton CP School, Honiton

Animal Alphabet

A mazing, attractive ant.
B rilliant, beautiful butterfly.
C ute, cuddly cat.
D ozy, dopey dog.
E xcellent, exciting elephant.
F unky, frightened frog.
G orgeous, giggling giraffe.
H ungry, hunched horse.
I ncredible, interesting insect.
J umping, jiggling jellyfish.
K icking, killing kangaroo.
L azy, luscious lion.
M ischievous, mysterious monkey.
N asty, naughty nit.
O bedient, open octopus.
P eaceful, picky penguin.
Q uiet, quaint quail.
R unning, rampaging rhino.
S livering, scaly snake.
T iny, talented tadpole.
U nique, understanding umbrella fish.
V icious, violent vulture.
W onderful, whistling whale.
Y oung, yonder yak.
Z ooming, zigzag zebra.

Jasmine Jefferson (11)
Honiton CP School, Honiton

The Moon

The full moon is like a silky, silver mirror
Like a bright bottle top.
The full moon is like an asteroid
Bouncing to Earth.
The full moon is like an egg
That's got bumps on it.
The full moon is like a ping-pong ball
That's being hit from the sun to Earth.
It is as shiny as silver.
The full moon is like a golf ball
Being hit from Pluto into a hole.
It's as sparkly as a sparkler.

Jack Dare (8)
Honiton CP School, Honiton

Brothers And Sisters

Mysterious smirks on their faces,
My brother and sister.
Scattering to different places,
As annoying as a blister.

Silly songs they sing,
Singing is all they do.
Made up words that don't make sense,
They don't have a clue.

Hiding my things around the house,
Sticking my homework together like a giant tube.
Sneaking like a little mouse,
As I catch them they freeze like an ice cube.

The best thing about them,
Is that they are quiet when they are asleep.
All you hear is peace and quiet,
They don't make a peep.

Abbie Villiers (10)
Honiton CP School, Honiton

The Winning Four

I am going to explode
I can't wait anymore
The fielders are dashing
Through that door.
I hit it, hard and strong
To the boundary wall
The bowler shots fiercely
To catch the ball.
The ball punches
Through the sky
Like a rocket into space
I watch it fly.
The fielder is sprinting like a cheetah
Running viciously to catch his prey
To save a winning four
But I win the day!

Foyezur Rahman (11)
Honiton CP School, Honiton

Desert

The desert
Like a sandstorm
Twisting strongly
Across the plains.

Lizards travelling
Through the desert
Camouflaged by the sand.
Its rough skin ready to fall.

You can see many cacti nearby
They are prickly
The desert is dry
Hot and hostile.

Christopher Stamp (11)
Honiton CP School, Honiton

Friends Are Best!

Friends are best
They're there for me
They remind me of little stars!

You love them
They love you
Just be together, just forever
Everyone's my friend!

We have sleepovers
Brush our hair
Paint our nails
And do dares!

Friends are best
They're there for me
They remind me of little stars
I hope they think of me this way too!

Friends!

Hannah Chapman (11)
Honiton CP School, Honiton

The Full Moon

The full moon is like a ping-pong ball
Bouncing down to Earth like a meteor
Coming down from space.

The full moon is like a clock ticking every second.

The full moon is like an eyeball
Spying when you are asleep.

The full moon is like a crystal ball
Shining in the sky.

Charlie Stephenson (8)
Honiton CP School, Honiton

The Fight . . .

The fist rose up furiously,
Tension grew,
Stressed . . . I hit him,
Anger flew.

I hurt the person,
He suffered . . . pain,
He cried with emotion,
I hit him again.

They split the destruction,
Between him and me,
Fury fired up,
We broke free.

The last moments of the fight,
I'm out of stress,
Fighting becomes a habit,
Crying in sadness.

I had a sorrowful moment.

Matthew Baker (11)
Honiton CP School, Honiton

The Full Moon

The full moon is like a crystal ball
Floating somewhere in one polluted atmosphere.
The full moon is forced to beam
By the scorching sun.
The beaming by day is much more powerful than night.
The full moon is like a golf ball
Being whacked by the asteroid belt.

Matthew Trechmann (8)
Honiton CP School, Honiton

What About?

What about -
The small spider
Squashed one day
Not a good hider?

What about -
The buzzing bee
Stings one day
Dies for all to see?

What about -
The fiery fox
Slain one day
For fur in a box?

What about -
The docile duck
Shot one day
Doesn't have much luck?

What about -
The human race
Killed every day
To keep us in place?

Emma Weir (11)
Honiton CP School, Honiton

The Cup Final

The crowd flood in
Like a pack of wolves
Hoping their team will win.
They all take a seat
Moaning and groaning
Or they get something to eat.
The game begins
As the whistle blows
What will happen if Millwall wins?

One-nil Man U take the lead
That's not a surprise
Thanks to Giggs' great speed.
Oh no, they've equalised
That's a surprise
Even though they're not specialised.
We try to get it back
Which should be easy
But they just wouldn't lack.

Here comes Giggsy
Millwall should fear.
Aww, that's a penalty
They hope to be in the clear.
The crowd silently pause
As they wait for the shot.
Nistelrooy shoots, he scores.
The whistle has gone
For the final time.
Man United have won.

Aaron King (11)
Honiton CP School, Honiton

Dolphins

They move swiftly,
Along the rough waves,
Screeching and moaning,
For days and days,
Their peaceful faces,
Their splashing,
Along the waves these things take place.

Sometimes they feel free,
Sometimes they feel happy,
But no one knows,
Their deepest, deepest secret.

Diving into the deepest sea,
Not knowing what they will find,
But one day, one day,
The world will close on them,
Like a net over their eyes.

Gracefully moving,
Swimming swiftly,
Blowing water, silently and triumphant,
Swift as they are,
Not knowing what to think,
About the killer humans.

Lydia Heaven (11)
Honiton CP School, Honiton

Midnight

At midnight
When you're asleep,
You hear the owl
Gliding by,
The howling of the wolf,
The trees moving.

At midnight
There's blackness around,
The moon rises
In the dark, night sky,
With the stars above
Shining like small, circular specks.

At midnight
Clashing lightning appears,
With a powerful scream
Carrying a thunderous roar.

At midnight
It's not night-time now.
Darkness fades,
Up comes the sun,
Rising.

Isobel Dobson (11)
Honiton CP School, Honiton

Horses

The hooves crushing through
The long, thick grass.
Its mane blowing past,
The horse's bold eyes widening.
Its beautiful markings glistening
In the bright sun.
Its velvet nose sniffing for food
In the long, thick grass!
The horse's gallop is as mighty
As a lion's roar!
Hooves clashing and stamping,
Destroying the long, thick grass.
The horse is snorting,
Its nostril's are flaring.
Its hair damp and wet
Through the hot, summer's day
In the long, thick grass!

Kirsty Sanders (10)
Honiton CP School, Honiton

My Cousins

My cousins eat my food,
They hate getting told off,
They are rather rude,
They sulk like a moth.

My cousins hate having a kiss,
They headbutt me into bed,
But they always miss,
And I hit my head.

My cousins don't kick or punch,
They love polishing and cleaning,
They love making lunch,
I love them with meaning.

Ben Bright (11)
Honiton CP School, Honiton

The Moon

The moon is like a crystal ball
Looking down on the Earth
Like a white eye
Staring at you.

The moon is like a football
Being kicked to the centre of the Earth
Like a torpedo
Being shot out of nowhere.

The moon is like a whizzing frisbee
Rolling like the moon
Falling to the sea
Like a gigantic roll swaying to my mouth.

The moon is like a piece of cheese
Waiting to be eaten!

Niall Boulton (8)
Honiton CP School, Honiton

Weather

On a horrible day,
Clouds are coming in from over the west.
It's starting to rain,
On the windowpane.

Puddles form like teardrops,
Children splashing puddles in a bath.
Thunder and lightning,
Crashing, it's frightening.

The wind is taking side to side,
Whispers secrets to children.
Children are sleeping,
While the wind is creeping.

Lauren Strutt (11)
Honiton CP School, Honiton

Monsters In The Dark

When I'm in bed
I hear footsteps on the stairs
It stops
Then there are footsteps in the hall.

I think of happy thoughts
But I keep on hearing footsteps
I put my head under the covers
It jumps on my bed, I move, it runs away.

It tries to get in my sister's room
It holds on to the handle
It lets go
Bang! I think it fell over.

It runs to my mum and dad's room
I look, there's nothing there
I hear it coming
I put my head back under the covers.

In the morning I go downstairs
Something's following me
I stop, turn around
The cat is following me!

Alex Gocher (10)
Honiton CP School, Honiton

Why?

I was over at a party,
had a couple of drinks.
I didn't know I was drunk,
I just didn't think.

There I was,
just gulping it down,
drop after drop,
I didn't frown.

I stepped in the car,
that night at midnight
and to my surprise
I saw a bright light.

All of a sudden I awoke
in a lonely hospital bed.
my mum told me what happened,
this is what she said . . .

'You were driving faster than fast,
screeched on the brakes too late,
you crashed into a tree,
we didn't know your fate.'

I gasped and cried,
'Thank goodness it was a tree.
could you imagine
if it was you or me?'

Danielle Wakley (11)
Honiton CP School, Honiton

Super Duper Family!

Your family might be perfect,
Your family might be brilliant,
Your family might be the best,
But my family are the best out of the rest.

My family, dad, mum, sis and bro,
And the great me,
Are a super duper family.
Can I repeat that?
Are a super duper family.

Dad's a hardworking farmer,
Mum's a loving housewife,
Brother George is annoying but cool,
And he's only seven,
Sister Zosha, a Polish name, very cute,
And coming up two.

And then there's me,
Coming up twelve,
The best out of the three.

My family, dad, mum, sis and bro,
And the great me,
Are a super duper family.
Can I repeat that?
A super duper family.

Shannon Croton (11)
Honiton CP School, Honiton

Forest Of Fear

I stride through the forest,
My head bowed down,
My confused mind turning,
Turning round and round.

I stumbled over the forest roots,
Sprawled along the ground,
Like snakes scattered here and there,
I'm alone, there's not a sound.

The forest's carpet is brown and dusty,
A cluster of mud and twigs,
Like milkshake powder surrounding me,
Fir trees, oaks and figs.

I'm following an endless path,
Trees on either side of me,
They're covered by clinging moss,
Like a mother hugging her baby.

I can hear sounds around me,
Sounds I don't want to hear,
Werewolves, foxes and other monsters,
That I hope aren't here.

Holly Ainsworth (11)
Honiton CP School, Honiton

The Full Moon

The moon is white, silvery-grey,
Staring down at you,
It beams like a silvery plate
Shining bright.

People think the moon makes you go crazy,
People think the moon is a lump of cheese!
Then it's grey like a cloud
And red like fire, flaming bright

The full moon is like a crystal ping-pong ball,
Of grey silver marble,
Like a shining disco ball
Lighting up rainbow colours in the night.

People think there is a man in the moon,
They think it's got a face on it!
But it's just a silver bottle top
Suspended above the galaxy!

Laura Woollacott (8)
Honiton CP School, Honiton

The Full Moon

The full moon is like a ping-pong ball
Shining down from a window like a white balloon.

The full moon is like a golf ball
Thrown from the window as a circle.

The full moon is like a cooker plate
Shining down from a window like a white ball.

Yasmin Miller (7)
Honiton CP School, Honiton

The Full Moon

The full moon spies down like a creepy thief
Peering through the clouds
Like a ping-pong ball
Bouncing around the night's sky.

The full moon is like a crystal ball
Reflecting light to the Earth
Like the sudden light of a torch.

The full moon is like a silvery plate
Smashing down to Earth
Like a disco light.

The full moon is like a bottle top
Twirling around the night sky
Like a firefly.

Amy Shawyer (7)
Honiton CP School, Honiton

The Moon

The moon is like a ping-pong ball sitting on a cloud.
The moon rises in its own time;
Dream, lying in the moon's curve feeling just like cheese inside.
An egg is like the moon and rolls the same.
If an egg cracks the moon could too.
The full moon is like a biscuit flying towards my mouth
Like a bomb dropped over enemy territory.
The moon is like my head rolling around in the sky
Wherever I go the moon follows.
The crescent moon is like a boomerang
Coming back from space.
The crescent moon is half eaten.

Harriet Morris (8)
Honiton CP School, Honiton

The Full Moon

The full moon is like a golf ball
Flying in mid-air
Like an alien spacecraft
Flying over you.

The full moon is like a frisbee
Zooming over the land
Like an asteroid
Raining down on you.

The full moon is like a clock face
Staring at the galaxy.

The full moon is a football
Kicking into the galaxy goal.

The full moon is like a pale face
Spitting, spitting
Like a cobra.

Matthew Richards (8)
Honiton CP School, Honiton

Nine Things Found In A Dragon Slayer's Pocket

A green scale from a dragon he slayed.
A pure fire tear trying to return to the earth.
A spark of flame in a bottle.
A baby dragon frozen in time.
An egg stolen from a dragon's nest.
The fearlessness in a dragon's eye.
The pure, golden heart of the last true dragon.
A droplet of ice fire trying to restore the dragon it came from.
The pure white canine of a dragon that's escaped.

Bethany Parsons (10)
Ilfracombe CE Junior School, Ilfracombe

Ten Things Found In A Ballerina's Pocket

A pair of ballet shoes
Which were all worn out from dancing.

A brown hairnet
To put her hair up in a bun.

Four hairpins for each side
Which were all bent out of shape.

A lovely pink suit
All scrunched up in a bundle.

A CD
With slow, graceful music on it.

An extra lace
In case she falls over and one snaps.

A pair of light pink tights
To match her pink suit.

A bottle of water
For when she gets thirsty.

A hair band
To put her hair up in different styles.

Some make-up for the show.

Fay Ackfield-Case (9)
Ilfracombe CE Junior School, Ilfracombe

Winter

W hite mornings when you can see your breath.
 I ce lays on tree branches.
N ice white snow swiftly falling.
T rees are slowly losing their leaves.
E ating snowflakes as they fall.
R unning through crunchy, frozen leaves.

Gina Bryant (9)
Ilfracombe CE Junior School, Ilfracombe

The Window

There once was a very small window
Hidden away in the corner of the room.

One day a barmaid looked through the window
And saw a delicious pint.

 A baker looked through the window
And saw a tasty cake.

A monkey looked through the window
And saw a bunch of glossy, new bananas.

A dog looked through the window
And saw a big, juicy bone.

 A zombie looked through the window
And saw a shiny, smooth coffin.

A builder looked through the window
And saw a great house ready to sell.

I looked through the window
And saw world peace.

Matthew McKee (9)
Ilfracombe CE Junior School, Ilfracombe

Ten Things In A Teenager's Pocket

A full secret diary,
A kiss from a last boyfriend,
The thought of a date,
A folder full of homework,
A mobile full of boys' numbers,
An annoying little brother,
A romantic poem,
A sparkling golden chain,
A model magazine,
A picture of a lover.

Sofia Vicente (9)
Ilfracombe CE Junior School, Ilfracombe

You!

You!
Your chest is like a broken drum.
You!
Your lungs are like rasping balloons.
You!
Your arms are like a flailing whip.
You!
Your knees are like a creaking hinge.
You!
Your hair is like a hundred rats' tails.
You!
Your eyes are like a scarlet flame.
You!
Your toes are like gnarled tree branches.
You!
Your teeth are like cracked rose quartz.
You!
Your fingers are like blunt, rusty nails.
You!
Your brain is like a shrinking sponge.
So's yours, hmf!

Rachel Threlkeld & Beth Parsons (10)
Ilfracombe CE Junior School, Ilfracombe

A Question?

What would life be without the world, space or anything?
It would be nothing.
What's nothing?
What does nothing look like?
What is the meaning of life?
What is the meaning of death?
Think about it.

Jack Turner & Daniel Barbeary (11)
Ilfracombe CE Junior School, Ilfracombe

Window

There once was a very small window
Hidden away in the corner of a room.

One day a doctor looked through the window
And saw a healthy patient.

A swimmer looked through the window
And saw a golden medal.

Henry VIII looked through the window
And saw his six wives.

A dog looked through the window
And saw a juicy bone.

A cat looked through the window
And saw a huge tin of fish.

A football player looked through the window
And saw the World Cup.

I looked through the window
And saw my best friend.

Sarah Campbell (9)
Ilfracombe CE Junior School, Ilfracombe

Ten Things Found In A Fairy's Pocket

A purse full of fairy dust
A magic wand with powers
A letter from the wind
A picture of the sky
A magic talking star
A power to fly
A stone to heal
A box of jewels
A song for the sun
A story of magic.

Caitlin Robertson (10)
Ilfracombe CE Junior School, Ilfracombe

My Cat

My cat is . . .
always sleeping
sometimes creeping
bird catching
claw scratching
eyes stunning
fast running
whiskers twitching
ears pricking
tongue licking
paws skipping
always eating
sometimes pleading
tail wagging
belly hanging
fight losing
private pooing
mouse murdering
and purring
always prowling
and miaowing
sort of a cat!

Katy McCarten (10)
Ilfracombe CE Junior School, Ilfracombe

Winter

W hen the sky is full of clouds.
I cy floor, so had to walk on.
N ow people come outside to make a snowman.
T ouching frosty leaves.
E tching patterns are formed by raindrops.
R eaching for a snowflake.

Naomi Dymond-Drury (10)
Ilfracombe CE Junior School, Ilfracombe

School

Watching the clock 6 hours a day,
Running straight out to play.

Changing into shorts and T-shirts,
Changing from jumpers and skirts.

Waiting for lunch in a line,
Looking at the rain, waiting for sunshine.

Literacy, writing a story,
History, horrible and gory!

Hometime, hooray, yippee!
Time to act like a chimpanzee!

But remember tomorrow will be the same as today
So make the most of free time and go out and play!

Abigail Barter (10)
Ilfracombe CE Junior School, Ilfracombe

Don't

Don't cook the kettle.
Don't bath the cat.
Don't eat slugs and snails.
Don't walk like that.

Don't write on eggs.
Don't bathe in ink.
Don't paint the wallpaper.
Don't sleep in the sink.

Don't draw on your face.
Don't eat the door.
Don't water the table leg.
Don't butter the floor.

Ella Mawson (8)
Ilfracombe CE Junior School, Ilfracombe

What Is Hot?

Chilli peppers
Morning toast
An electric shock
Sunday roast.

A glowing light
Steam from a kettle
Flame from a fire
A stinging nettle.

Sizzling sausages
Sand on a sunny day
Peppermints
The sun's rays.

Hot water bottle
Sparklers when they stop
Drinking chocolate
Running to the shop.

Megan Barnes (8)
Ilfracombe CE Junior School, Ilfracombe

Nine Things Found In A Ghost's Pocket

A picture of his family that are living without him.
A sausage he kept from the last meal he could ever eat.
The bullet that killed him.
A flower he picked off his grave.
The memory of his killer's face.
A wooden pole he carries to get revenge on his killer.
A compass to lead him to the ghost ship.
A map of Ghost Land.
A dream to live again.

Lauren Burge (10)
Ilfracombe CE Junior School, Ilfracombe

Without You

Without you
I'm like a butterfly without wings,
An aeroplane without air,
Or a marriage without rings.

Without you
I'm like a clock without hands
For whatever you do
I always understand.

Lee Holden (11)
Ilfracombe CE Junior School, Ilfracombe

Who Is It?

Who saved my sister at the hospital?
Who saved my family from a fire?
Who saved my house from being burgled?
Who are they, who are they?
Who saved my pet bird?
Who taught me my first word?
Who taught me to add 2+2?
Who made my house?
Who is it, who is it?
We might never know.
We might never see them again.
But thank them if you do.
It might just make their day.
So lend a hand and you could save someone's life.

Charlotte Campbell (11)
Ilfracombe CE Junior School, Ilfracombe

Winter

As our warm breath floats up in the air
The tree peels in the winter
With the frost falling from the sky.

Adam Smith (10)
Ilfracombe CE Junior School, Ilfracombe

My Cat Tickles

My cat Tickles
Likes to eat cheese
My cat Tickles
Creates catastrophes
My cat Tickles
Has loads of fun
Playing in the hot, summer sun
My cat Tickles
Is really cool
My cat Tickles
Dives in the pool
My cat Tickles
Makes me smile
Watching her play
All the while
My cat Tickles
Is really great
That is why
She's my best mate.

Alicia Fay (10)
Ilfracombe CE Junior School, Ilfracombe

My Dad

My dad's cool
My dad's kind
My dad's cheerful all the time
My dad's great
My dad's my mate
My dad's someone I do not hate
My dad's fun
He annoys my mum
If he has a cake he would eat every crumb!

And that's my dad!

Jordan Davey (11)
Ilfracombe CE Junior School, Ilfracombe

Spirit Of A Horse

It's great to be wild so you can run free,
So jump on my back and you will see,
We'll gallop across the sandy plains,
And they'll say, 'Hey, wait for me.'

Once we've galloped across the plains,
Will you look after me, please?
Don't worry, I'll tell you what to do,
All I need is love and attention then we'll get through.

Muck, muck, horrible muck,
Muck, muck, smelly muck,
Quick, quick, get rid of that *muck.*

Feed, feed, glorious feed,
Feed, feed, yummy feed,
Quick, quick, must eat the *feed.*

Tack, tack, beautiful tack,
Tack, tack, clean tack,
Tack, tack, *tack me up.*

Groom, groom, groom, I'm dirty now,
Groom, groom, groom me now,
Quick, quick, *until I shine.*

Emily Wells (10)
Ilfracombe CE Junior School, Ilfracombe

Nine Things Found In A Teenager's Pocket

A brand new mobile phone
A bright red lipstick that she wears every day
A pink diary which all her secrets are in
A homework diary full but never finished
An old piece of chewing gum that she chews in nervous times
A hair brush just in case she meets a boy
A picture of her boyfriend when he was a baby
A piece of paper with her boyfriend's lips printed on it
A hand-written guide to romance.

Kelsey Jackson (9)
Ilfracombe CE Junior School, Ilfracombe

Looking After Your Pony

Hop on my back, we'll have a ball
We'll gallop through fields
From sunrise to sun fall
So hold on tight
And do not fright
For I shall protect you with all my might.

All I ask of you
Is that you treat me as I would you
Make sure I'm fed
And make my bed
Then groom me in the morning.

So if you care for me
I shall never flee.

I will take a glorious stride
As we ride.

I will stay with you until the end
For you are
My only friend.

Katrina Bryant (11)
Ilfracombe CE Junior School, Ilfracombe

Beach

I love playing on the beach,
With the wind and waves at my reach,
The waves come crashing with the tide,
Waiting to get on my board and have a ride.
I go rock-pooling and catch a fish,
I have it for dinner on my dish.
I sit on my pink towel having an ice cream,
I look up at the sky having a dream.
I walk along the beach and have a roam,
I look at my watch, it's now time to go home!

Kelly Davison (10)
Ilfracombe CE Junior School, Ilfracombe

Winter Trees

Dark bark all bumpy and brown,
Standing like statues,
Waving their long, bare twigs in the air.

Whirly, prickly branches,
Reaching up to the sky.

Pointing up to the sky,
Waiting patiently for spring.

The trunk so fat,
It looks like a tall chimney pot.

Patterns on the bark,
Swirly and whirly.

Reaching up to the sky,
Like an acrobat stretching.

Jessica Hornsby (8)
Ilfracombe CE Junior School, Ilfracombe

Winter Trees

Sharp twigs stretching
in the cold wind,
skinny fingers pointing
into the sky.

The sharp twigs
wide and wavy,
the tree trunk
is crooked and cold.

Patterns on the tree trunk
crinkly and rough,
trees dancing in the wind,
floating in the air.

Twigs pointing into the air,
sharp branches waving
in the cold, rough wind.

Chloe Huelin (8)
Ilfracombe CE Junior School, Ilfracombe

Winter Trees

Branches pointing like fingers
Into the sky,
Like an acrobat stretching up high.
Twirly twigs, big and small,
Prickly branches waving their fingers,
Pointing up tall into the sky.
Trees dancing in the wind,
Waving their branches.
Trees rustling in the wind,
Like leaves crunching.
Still statues bendy and wobbly.

Sophie Campbell (8)
Ilfracombe CE Junior School, Ilfracombe

A Recipe For Winter

Mix together some glistening ice,
Some frozen water,
As hard as iron,
And some soft, mushy snow.
Take some lethal-looking trees,
Two teaspoons of frosty grass,
And an ounce of snowmen,
With coal buttons,
And a carrot nose.
Add some broken conkers lying in the snow,
Some excited children playing,
And some church bells ringing.
Decorate with sparkling, white tinsel,
Some carol singers,
Singing at the tops of their voices,
And some shiny mistletoe.
Leave for three months and you have made winter.

Joseph Borthwick (9)
Keyham Barton Catholic Primary School, Plymouth

Fox

I was on a school trip,
When,
Out of a rustling bush,
Appeared a sly fox.

Moving his tail slightly,
In the wispy breeze,
It turned its head,
Looking straight at me.

I looked at him,
And his wide, yellow eyes,
Glared back at me,
It opened its mouth,
Exposing lots of long, sharp teeth.

Then it howled,
As loud as a trumpet,
As piercing as a scream,
And horrible, salivary slime,
Dribbled down the side of its mouth.

I stood,
Transfixed,
As a huge surge of jealousy,
Erupted inside me,
I wish I could be a fox,
Cunning,
Sly,
And sharp-eyed.

Peter Jerrett (9)
Keyham Barton Catholic Primary School, Plymouth

Alligator

Down by the muddy swamp,
I saw a long, camouflaged alligator.
He swung his long, wet, spiky tail
Into the swamp.
Soon
All I could see
Was his spiky, camouflaged back.
The points of his spikes
Were like the tips of forks,
Sharp and pointed.

He was so powerful.
His eyes looked deeply at the trees
And then,
As if by magic,
He disappeared
But
Under the dark, still water
You could see his tail whip from side to side
And his mouth snapping.

I felt my blood swirling up inside me.
My nerves were drawing near.
I panicked in fear
But before I knew it
He was gone
Leaving a ripple path
Where he glided out of sight
But not out of mind.

Niamh O'Connell (9)
Keyham Barton Catholic Primary School, Plymouth

Mauritius Wind

I pulled granules of sand up high from the beach.
I dropped them on a rock.
I made the grains twist and twirl.
I pushed a beach ball through the sea.
I hurried back through the beach.
I swooped a newspaper out of someone's hand.
I lifted it high up into the sky.
I broke a coconut from its tree.
I snapped a piece of sugar cane from its field.
I became weaker,
So weak that people didn't know I was there.

Harvey Parsons (8)
Keyham Barton Catholic Primary School, Plymouth

Recipe For Winter

Take some carrot-nosed snowmen,
Some sprinkles of snowflakes
And some fog.
Add some dark, short days,
Some black skies
And some sparkling stars.
Mix with roast turkey,
Some Yorkshire puddings
And some roast potatoes.
Decorate with flickering flames,
Some hot cocoa
And chestnuts.
Leave for three whole months
And you have winter.

Amber Seymour (9)
Keyham Barton Catholic Primary School, Plymouth

A Siberian Tiger

I saw it!
A black and white tiger, a Siberian tiger
Curling its claws.

It moved with a slashing claw.
I gazed in a trance of amazement
As it pounced onto a gazelle.
My blood turned cold.
I felt a ball of jealousy crawl up my brain.
I desperately wanted to be a Siberian tiger.

Suddenly the tiger pounced!
It landed with a thump and a bump right next to me.
I hid under a pile of leaves.
At least it think they were leaves.
Suddenly
A wispy wind tornadoed at the leaves
As if tackling them.
The leaves raced off me.
Charging to battle
They swept away.
Luckily for me
The Siberian tiger had disappeared.

William Ashfield (9)
Keyham Barton Catholic Primary School, Plymouth

Hobbies

Piano is fun to learn
Using my fingers on the keys
To play the notes
To play a melody.

Running as fast as the wind
To become fitter and better
Legs like lightning
Across the fields of green.

Gymnastics, bending bodies
Handstands, cartwheels and forward rolls
Twisting, turning in every direction
Balancing on wooden beams.

Athletics is great for the muscles
Three-legged races with your partner
Various obstacles to hop, skip and jump over
Relays to be won.

Hobbies that give you
    Talent!

Rebecca Trethewey (11)
Ladock CE Primary School, Truro

Cheetahs

As fast as the wind,
As cunning as a fox,
Roaring,
Pouncing,
In the wilderness.
As fast as the wind,
As cunning as a fox.
Cheetahs!

Caitlin Mulroy (10)
Ladock CE Primary School, Truro

The Snake And The Mouse

A grass snake slithers softly through the grass
Watching and spying on its prey.
The field mouse pops his head up in fear.
Still in the grass the snake lies still.
The tiny mouse trembles and sees the snake
Then he scurries away.
The snake hisses and the field mouse fights
And attempts to bite the snake's tail.
The mouse misses so the snake attacks again.
The poor injured mouse, still and silent,
On the ground with blood coming out from its head.
The snake swallows it in one big bite.
I hope all other mice run faster than this mouse
To their safe nest.

Joseph Moore (11)
Ladock CE Primary School, Truro

Dead Or Alive

A secret doorway
A mysterious stair
A heap of fungi
As long as hair
Long passed stumps
With ever a dare.

A life of Heaven
For those long passed
With birds and squirrels
And bones all gnashed
With the Devil ever fighting
The trees of yew.

Skeletons and birds
Stars in herds
Dead or alive?

Ryan Goodwin (11)
Luxulyan School, Bodmin

I Wish I Was . . .

A butterfly with all the pretty colours on my wings
Flapping to stay floating above the horizon.
A skydiver being able to jump out of an aeroplane
And seeing all the beautiful views from above.
A bird being able to judge the length between me
                              and the sensitive ground.
A crocodile with long, sharp teeth snapping at predators.
A hamster being able to run around in circles in its wheel.

Heather Charlesworth (10)
Luxulyan School, Bodmin

I Wish I Was . . .

A colossal white shark swimming in the sea.
A fierce lion roaring in the jungle.
A beautiful swan sleeping in the lake.
A speedy car zooming up the track to win.
A gorilla swinging from tree to tree.
A huge dinosaur fighting extinction in the land of Oz.
A bull in a field stampeding at a red cloth.
An aggressive dog living in a zoo.

Jessica Bone (11)
Luxulyan School, Bodmin

I Wish I Was A . . .

Sparkling star hovering in the dark night sky,
Moon staring down on the sparkling stars,
Bird looking for a comfy space to land,
Buzzard darting down for the fish in the sea,
Owl hooting in the dark night sky,
Butterfly with a symmetrical pattern on its wings.

Emily Andrews (11)
Luxulyan School, Bodmin

The Churchyard

The aged gate standing strong like a grown man prepared for battle
Chopped wood lying like dead soldiers on the grass of green
Graves in the shape of pyramids with lichen crawling up to the top
Bluebells peeking, waiting to be noticed
A monkey puzzle tree sprouting so speedy that's now the tallest tree
Buttercups reaching out the soil like they've just awoken
The sun glimmering on the ancient grave
Beech nuts firm on the ground with tall trees towering above
Acres of land with graves and other objects attached.

Steven Hooper (10)
Luxulyan School, Bodmin

The Valley

A carpet of autumn colours
Trees bare and lifeless
Moss crawls up the ancient trunks
Mine shaft lies deep underground.

Trees bare and lifeless
Battered tram track from long ago
Mine shaft lies deep underground
Heron silently stalking his prey.

Battered tram track from long ago
Icy cold river gushing against rocks
Heron silently stalking his prey
Squirrel stashing nuts for winter.

Icy cold river gushing against rocks
Holly berries as red as blood
Squirrel stashing nuts for winter
Bird's nest camouflaged in the tree.

Shannon Fahey (10)
Luxulyan School, Bodmin

The Valley

Beech tree trunks as smooth as silk.
Squirrels leaping from tree to tree.
Fungi creeping up the rough bark.
Rabbits springing through the grass.

Ashley Hick (9)
Luxulyan School, Bodmin

Haiku

A woodland valley
Squirrels racing up the trees
Sunlight on the leaves.

Eddie George (7)
Luxulyan School, Bodmin

Haiku

A small hidden stream
Beyond beautiful valleys
Water glistening.

Shaun Pickering (11)
Luxulyan School, Bodmin

Haiku

Among the bushes
Hidden there was a bluebell
It stood all alone.

Luke Rowe (10)
Luxulyan School, Bodmin

I Wish I Was . . .

A crispy leaf tumbling to the ground.
A friendly dolphin devouring fish
A horse stampeding through the lush, green grass.
A playful puppy lying in the dazzling sun
An immense airplane zooming through the sunset sky.

Lauren Hoskin (9)
Luxulyan School, Bodmin

My Dad

My dad is brill
He's just a thrill
He takes me places
Seeing wonderful faces
He cares for me
Whilst having his tea
We saw a snake
As it ate its bait
He's really fun
And is number 1.

Jessica Haley (11)
Mount Charles CP School, St Austell

My Horse

My horse is very sweet,
She lets me wash and clean her feet,
She likes her food and lots of hay,
And with her friends she will run and play.

I ride her fast, I ride her slow,
Wherever I ask she will go,
We have won rosettes and prizes galore,
Duchess, you are the best horse I could ask for.

Chaela Richmond (9)
Mount Charles CP School, St Austell

Night

The sun goes down
To reveal the heavens
As the day turns to night.

Her million eyes shine
Like newly-cut diamonds
As the day turns to night.

The owl's sweet song
Plays the same sweet tune
In the midnight breeze
As day turns to night.

The trees sway side to side
Like dreaming dancers
As day turns to night.

Her eyes start to shut
One by one
The moon starts to go
The sun's starting to rise
As night turns to day.

Danny Allum (10)
Mount Charles CP School, St Austell

Horse Wishes

I wish I had a horse,
Her brown mane shimmering in the light.
I'd ride her every day,
And stay with her at night.

I would love to groom, muck out and ride,
And when she gallops,
I would ride aside.
I wish I had a horse!

Jamileh Clifford (10)
Mount Charles CP School, St Austell

Ma Hamster Honey

Ma hamster - Honey,
Elle est trés trés - funny.
Ses pieds sont - pink,
Et par fois - stink!
Ses dents sont - scary,
Et me faire - wary.
Elle se tient dans le - cage,
Elle est pleine de - rage,
L'attente à - bite,
Et me donner un - fright!

Hannah Salisbury (11)
Mount Charles CP School, St Austell

A Recipe For A Flower

Take a sweet smell
Mix some pretty little petals
Bake a stigma, a stem
And some leaves will do.
Crumble the stamen
And then the style.
Stir some seeds to help it grow
And now you've made a
Flower
So leave
It to
Grow!

Lily Richardson (8)
Mount Charles CP School, St Austell

Best Friends

Best friends always stick together
They tell each other secrets
They do everything side by side
They make each other bracelets.

But they don't hurt each other
They don't let each other down
They don't make faces
They don't give a frown.

Georgia Haywood (8)
Mount Charles CP School, St Austell

Whale-Shark At School

I came across a whale-shark
On the way to school.
His tusks were very hot
And his hairstyle very cool.
I hid him in my PE bag
So the teacher would not see.
He stayed there very silently
Until frightened by a flea!

Sophie Marsh (7)
Mount Charles CP School, St Austell

Miss

Miss, can I go to the toilet, please?
Yes, you may.
Miss, I've finished my work.
Have you? *Wow!*
Miss, can I go out to play, please?
No, it's not playtime!
Miss, can I go home, please?
No, you have just started school!

Mark Borman (10)
Mount Charles CP School, St Austell

Madison's Swirly Zoo

Sally, the silly tiger, had swirls instead of stripes.
She had swirls on her nose
And even her toes,
Which showed right through her tights!

Lucy, the lucky monkey, had a very swirly tail.
She used it each day
To help her to play.
Her favourite game was 'Hunt the Snail'!

Hermione, the hungry giraffe, had a very swirly neck.
It helped her to eat leaves
That grew on the trees
But they made her feel a wreck!

Ronald, the roaring lion, had swirls all over his mane.
He thought he looked cool
But he was such a silly fool
And everyone thought the same!

These are the swirly animals that live in the swirly zoo.
The keeper is a girly
Whose dress is very swirly
And her name is Maddy Moo!

Madison Tellam (6)
Mount Charles CP School, St Austell

My Dog

Eyes-scary
Fur-knotted
Cat-catcher
Cat-hunter
Bed-bumper
Bone-taker
Big-mumbler
Tail-twitcher
Cat-flattener.

Chelsea Walker (9)
Mount Charles CP School, St Austell

The Picnic Tea

We found a warm spot under a tree,
Here's what we had for our picnic tea!

We had . . .
Ants in the apples,
Slugs in the spaghetti,
Worms in the waffles,
Termites in the tasty turkey,
Snails in the salad sandwiches,
Woodlice in the water,
Grasshoppers in the grapes,
Midgets in the melon!

Ross Schooley-Frame (7)
Mount Charles CP School, St Austell

The Picnic Tea!

We found a shady spot under a tree,
Here's what we had for our picnic tea!

Ladybird in a lemon,
Woodlice in the water,
Leeches in the lettuce leaves,
Worms in the waffles,
Grasshoppers in the grapes,
Butterflies in the butter,
Snails in the sausages!
That's what we had for our picnic tea.

Troy Trevains (7)
Mount Charles CP School, St Austell

The Picnic Tea

We found a hot spot under a tree,
Here's what we had for our picnic tea!

We had . . .
Mites in the melon,
Snails in the syrup,
Slugs in the salad sandwiches,
Ladybirds on the lettuce leaves,
Moths in the mangoes,
Woodlice in the waffles,
Butterflies in the bananas,
Flies in the fruit.

Robyn Cotillard (7)
Mount Charles CP School, St Austell

The Picnic Tea

We found a grassy spot under a tree,
Here's what we had for our picnic tea!

We had . . .
Butterflies on the bananas,
Snails in the salad,
Termites in the tomatoes,
Worms in the washing water,
Midges on the mangoes,
Wasps on the waffles,
Flies in the fromage,
Sweets full of slugs!

Isabella Snell (7)
Mount Charles CP School, St Austell

The Wood

Gooey, sticky, brown mud clinging tightly to sticks and stones,
Then drowning in slurpy custard.

Mouldy, brown, Brussels sprouts spurting proudly
From suspicious-looking dark tree trunks.

The sky was blue . . . dark blue
As dull as a whale just floating there
Waiting for something to happen.

All chilly and draughty
With frosty rain bubbles appearing out of nowhere
Filling the air and drenching flying birds' homes.

Little tiny creatures with great big shadows
Scuttering in the moonlight.

Gemma Haywood (10)
Mount Charles CP School, St Austell

Recipe For A Happy School

Begin with some bright classrooms,
Take a mixture of teachers,
Cover with a timetable,
Add a sprinkling of children,
Twist in some smart uniforms,
Stir gently.
Add some pencils, pens, books, rubber and pencil cases,
Mix together some smart shoes and school bags.
Finally, add some PE kits and some hardworking brains.

What do you have?
A happy school!

India McCarthy (9)
Mount Charles CP School, St Austell

School Days

A crowd of blue and lots of grey
Ready to start another day
Children running to and fro
Looking for a place to go
Teachers sorting things for the class
While the kids have a laugh
Lessons start with literacy
Followed by some history
Bell rings, time for play
Best part of the day
It's lunchtime now, brill!
Waiting for chips to grill
Smell of fish and taste of peas
Kids crying when they graze their knees
What's the time? It's 3.00
Everyone is ready to flop
Now it is the end of the day
Hip hip hooray!

Sophie Workman (10)
Mount Charles CP School, St Austell

What Is Life?

What is life?
Some say it's a river, a journey from start to finish,
Some say it's the wind, a bit lonely here and there,
Some say it's a mountain that can never be conquered,
Some say, 'What is the point of life?'
But I say it's love!
Because that's what makes a life last forever!

Sarah Pinder (10)
Mount Charles CP School, St Austell

Monkey

He has a plain, cuddly body with
Big googly eyes and he's
Everywhere,
He's your friend like
A real person,
The cute and cuddly,
Face is really cheeky,
Like Valerie's smile.
He is really crazy and
Really mad as well.
He has a beautiful
Small tail,
He swings
Through the
Thick trees and
Makes a
Loud sound,
My sound goes
Oooh
Oooh
Aaah
Aaah.

Valerie Stephens (9)
Mount Charles CP School, St Austell

Sparkles And Shines

What sparkles like the stars and shines like the moon?
Not Mars
Not Venus
Not the Earth but close.
It's water.
Water shines like the moon and sparkles like the stars.

Kyle Taylor (6)
Mount Charles CP School, St Austell

All In A Day

I tried hard to
Keep my trainers
Clean but . . .
Isn't mud fun!

I tried hard to
Keep my skirt
Clean but . . .
Isn't water fun!

I tried hard to
Keep my hair
In but . . .
Isn't flicking fun!

I tried hard to
Keep my tie
Clean but . . .
Isn't a pen fun!

Jasmine Combellack (8)
Mount Charles CP School, St Austell

My Mum

My mum is just like a star
Mums like her are precious and few
So always thank her for all that she does
She's shiny as a star
She's brainy as a professor
She's as lively as a kitten
She's as beautiful as a star.

Thomas Powell (9)
Mount Charles CP School, St Austell

My Street

My street is so nice,
There aren't any mice,
Because my cat's on the scene,
She likes them with clotted cream.
Sydney is her name
And she is so tame.
My friend Max is the best
Out of all the rest.
Oliver is a dog who lives near,
He always licks your ear.
I can't rest
Because my street is the best.
I love this street
Because every day I have a treat.
I love my mum
But I hate gum.
Pretend policeman, James,
Always plays games.
Jodie is Max's cousin -
I have about a dozen.
I love my dad.
I think he is mad.
I like the milkman,
He comes early, in a van.
My neighbours are so cool.
Matthew is a total fool.
A hamster Katherine has just bought,
I want one too - now that's a thought.
Everyone looks out for me.
What a lovely place to be!

Finn Branney (7)
Mount Charles CP School, St Austell

Life

What is life?

Life is like an endless stream,
It flows on and on.

Life is like a story book,
Enjoy it while it lasts.

Life is like a cooling drink,
Soothing it has to end some time.

Debbie Pantling (11)
Mount Charles CP School, St Austell

Senses Of The Sea And Shore

I can see the sea crashing against the cliff,
And white, frothy foam turning back into the flowing tide.

I can hear the sea crashing against the rocks,
Lapping on the shore and roaring in the cave.

I can feel the sand as smooth as a shell,
I can feel the sea pulling the sand from under my feet.

I can smell the salt in the seaweed on the shore,
And the scent of lavender on the cliffs high above me.

I can see the bright colours of the flowers on the rocky cliffs,
And hear my voice e cho in the dark cave,
And the seagulls' cries on the wind.
I can see white horses rearing up in the waves as they crash
onto the shore.

I can feel the warmth of the sun with my bare feet on the golden,
shimmering sand,
And see the sun flickering on the rippling water of the sea.

Treve Stock (9)
Mullion Primary School, Helston

The Sea Shore

I can see the sea with the foam on the front of the waves
And the seaweed washed up to shore
With the waves crashing against the rock.

I can feel the sea with a breeze on my face
And it is relaxing.

I can hear the waves crashing against the rocks
And the sea drum.

I can smell the sea with a salty taste up my nose.

Matt Fletcher (9)
Mullion Primary School, Helston

I Can See the Sea

I can see the sea,
It looks like galloping white horses, jumping,
It is a lovely aqua and emerald colour.

I can hear the sea,
It splashes and crashes against the rocks,
It laps the shore,
When it hits the rocks, it's like cannons going off.

I can smell the sea,
It smells of lavender and salt on my dinner.

I can feel the sea,
It feels like smooth, silky material
And it is very refreshing.

Heydon Dark (7)
Mullion Primary School, Helston

The Sea

I can see the sea, turquoise-blue
and emerald-green.

I can hear the sea, crashing on the rocks
and I hear people playing.

I can smell the sea, I smell salt in the sea
and fresh fish from the sea.

I can feel the sea, sometimes it's as cold as ice
and sometimes as hot as the sun.

Jack Sherlock (8)
Mullion Primary School, Helston

Sensing The Sea

I can see the sea
splashing through the rocks
when it's calm I think it's a lagoon.

When I hear the sea
it sounds like people splashing
up and down.

I can feel the sea
it is s as smooth as possible
when I jump in
it wriggles down my legs.

I can smell the sea
when I smell the sea
it smells like salt
on my chips.

Monica Rimmer (7)
Mullion Primary School, Helston

The Sea

You can feel the glittering sea
You can feel the snowy sea
You can feel the coldness of the sea.

You can see the sparkling sea
You can see the aqua-coloured sea
You can see the fish in the sea.

You can smell the sweet lavender of the sea
You can smell the sweet scent of the ocean
You can smell the sweetness of the sea.

You can hear waves of the big blue
You can hear ripples overlapping
You can hear fish swimming.

Jack Emmanuel (8)
Mullion Primary School, Helston

All At Sea

I can see the beautiful aqua sea,
It's crystal clear and as turquoise as a frog.
I can hear the bubbles in and out of the waves,
I can hear the horses jumping out of the waves.
I can hear the crashes of the waves falling down,
I can smell the salty water in the air.
The beautiful seaweed and the cold, icy scent.
I can feel the sea, it's really refreshing.
It's perfect!

Georgia Lewis (7)
Mullion Primary School, Helston

The Sea

I can see the sea as an aqua-blue,
That shines when the sun shines at it,
And emerald that shines glowingly.
I can hear the sea crashing against the rocks,
When it comes in, then comes out very gently.
I can smell the sea as a sour, salty kind.
I can feel the sea as lots of sequins in a pot,
And ice set on my fingers.

Matthew Rendall (8)
Mullion Primary School, Helston

All I Ask

All I ask is a perfect night
with a lovely star
on a planet very far.

In the morning sun
when the day's just begun
I go to play.

I meet my friend as I go to school
I see a bully and then some more.

I wake up from my dream
and that's the way I seem.

Kadi Lambert (9)
Mullion Primary School, Helston

The Storm

A storm is coming
The sea laps the shore in ripples of black.

A storm is coming
I can see the huge waves raging.

A storm is here
The once gentle waves are like volleys of arrows penetrating the
sand's armour.

A storm is here
It's like a war between the sand and the sea.

A storm has passed
The damage has been done.

A storm has passed
The waves are like ripples once more.

Another storm is here.

Simon Oliver (10)
Mullion Primary School, Helston

The Sea

I could hear the bird in the background,
I heard the waves roaring onto the rocks,
Never in my life have I heard such a lovely sound,
It's the deep, blue sea.

I ran down to bathe in the sand,
As smooth, as soft as can be,
Never have I wanted so much
To be right next to the sea.

Tom Piggott (10)
Mullion Primary School, Helston

The Storm

There is a storm at sea tonight
As the wind rages like a screaming tornado
And the sea crashes like a heavy earthquake
All the people walk back home.

There is a storm at sea tonight
As the lightning strikes the angry sea
And ruins its perfect turquoise
And the sea jumps, trying to catch the fierce lightning.

There is a storm at sea tonight
As the sea hurled the ships across its broad tummy
And rages, rearing up and charging at the muddy hill
It leaps across the harbour walls and settles in the bay.

There was a storm at sea last night
But at the end of the storm the water sounded like a trickling stream
And the boats settled again in the harbour
There was a storm at sea last night
But now it's over.

George Furber (9)
Mullion Primary School, Helston

The Rough Sea

The waves of the rough sea are like two rams crashing together
And the wind rushing through waves like a tornado
The sea is as powerful as two hurricanes
The currents are as deadly as World War II.

When the waves crash down onto the shore it's like an earthquake
The colours of the sea are turquoise and aqua-green
The sea is as blue as blueberry gum
The sharp, jagged rocks in the sea are as sharp as a sword.

Ben Wormington (10)
Mullion Primary School, Helston

The Moods Of The Sea

The sea was as green as the aqua-green lagoon,
Which crashed to the floor,
Making ripples of all shapes and sizes,
Which sounded like a sleepy lullaby.

As the sun appeared behind the rocks,
It made colour as bright as the stars,
The colours were pinky and peachy,
Which fascinated my eyes.

It glistened at night,
And breathed as it came in and out of the shore,
It sounded like a pack of wolves were charging,
As it drew closer it got louder and louder.

Cecily Cuff (10)
Mullion Primary School, Helston

How I See The Sea

Sometimes the sea is calm,
Sometimes the sea is rough,
Every time you go in the sea,
The sea's really tough.

The sea can be turquoise,
Sometimes it can be aqua,
Sometimes it is green,
Or can be any colour.

When you dive in the sea,
It can sometimes be cold,
But when you swim in the sea,
It will become much warmer.

When you get out of the sea,
You begin to shiver,
Until the sun begins to shine,
To make you feel much better.

Sophie Salter (10)
Mullion Primary School, Helston

I See The Sea

I see the sea as a big mystery
Trying to make everybody
Happy all the summer.

I see the sea as playful
And giddy, swallowing surf boarders
As they float by.

I see the sea as destructive
And black, smashing the ships
Like paper cups.

Chris Bloor (11)
Mullion Primary School, Helston

The First Time I Saw The Sea

The first time I saw the sea
I felt a bit guilty.

I never liked the sea before
The way the waves lap the shore.

The way the sea is crystal clear
And all the sounds you'd want to hear.

The hands of the sea grab the sand
What an artistic land!

Never in our lives would we want
To be without the sea.

Josh Billington (10)
Mullion Primary School, Helston

The Sea

As I drove to the seaside,
I saw the waves crashing against the rocks
Like a rampaging dragon.
The white froth jumped out of the sea
And hung on to the car like a fishing net.

As the car stopped a great swirling beast came up
And confronted us
The swirling beast was
A rampaging sandstorm.

The sea was a sapphire colour
While the rampaging dragon was digging itself
Into the hard rock.

Edward Sherlock (10)
Mullion Primary School, Helston

Sea Moods

I could hear the azure sea rippling onto a bed of sand,
I could see the waves swerve around the rocks,
I could hear people splashing in the sea,
I could smell the sweet seaweed,
I could, I could.

I could hear the waves crash against the cliffs and rocks,
I could see the tide coming in,
I could, I could.

Edward Walker (10)
Mullion Primary School, Helston

The Sea

The sound you hear
In your ear
When you're at the seaside
Is only lots of snorkelling librarians
Putting their finger to their lips and *sshhh!*

The pong that enters your nose
When you're at the seaside
Is only lots of cannibal sharks
Scoffing their fish and chips, *yum-yum!*

The froth you see
Is only Zeus, the god's toothpaste,
Fallen from the sky.

The lapping of the waves
That you feel when you're at the seaside
Is only an old sea serpent heavily breathing.

Now you know the truth about the sea
You should use this knowledge *wisely!*

Rosenwyn Reeve (11)
Mullion Primary School, Helston

The Sea

The waves swirl in and out of the caves
The sand stays the same
The waves crash against the rock with raw power.

The sand is carved in many shapes and sizes
The waves lash against the sands
The day has ended.

Joe Lugg (10)
Mullion Primary School, Helston

When I Look At The Deep, Aqua Sea . . .

When I look at the deep, aqua sea
I see beautiful horses jumping on the waves.

When I look at the deep, aqua sea
I see a person breathing onto the shore.

When I look at the deep, aqua sea
I see a stampede following the waves.

When I look at the deep, aqua sea
I hear the waves crashing on the rocks like a cymbal.
When I looked at the deep, aqua sea
I can taste in my mouth the sweet sea salt from the passing waves.

When I look at the deep aqua sea
I hear whales singing in the far away background.

When I look at the deep, aqua sea
I can taste trout I can see swimming happily.

Rio Curti (10)
Mullion Primary School, Helston

The Message Of The Sea

As I look at the sea
As the sun sets
The peachy colour
On the horizon strikes me
Like a whiplash.

As I stand in peace
On the seashore
I hear a choir singing
A spiritual awakening song to me
From the ocean deep.

Whilst I stand on the seashore
I feel like I am in a world
Full of tranquillity.

The message of the sea is coming to me!

Mark Leach (11)
Mullion Primary School, Helston

The Sea

When I put a shell to my ear
I hear the *sh-sh-sh* sound of the wind.
When I climb the gigantic rocks
I see the translucent sea for miles around.
When I go under the water
I feel like a mermaid swimming
With the fish.
When I sunbathe on the sand
I can smell the rich aroma of salt on my body.
When I leave the beach I wish I could stay
And live with the sand, the sea, the rocks and me.

Becky Sandford (10)
Mullion Primary School, Helston

Sunset

The sunset glitters on the surface,
Tide ripples on the shore,
Children paddling at the water's edge.

Fishermen fish on the cliff face,
Clumps of sea thrifts grow on rocks,
Boats sail past as they rise and fall.

The sun shimmers like diamonds,
Dolphins leap over the water,
People dive off the pier in the harbour.

The seals bob up and down,
Seagulls swoop down and nick pasties,
Children fish in the rock pools.

Hannah Richardson (11)
Mullion Primary School, Helston

Dragons

Dragons big,
Scaly, green,
Flies up high,
By us unseen.

Smokey nose,
Fiery breath,
Wings stretched tight,
Looking for death.

Spiky tail,
Searching eyes,
Talons are sharp,
Swoops in skies.

Gemma Wells (8)
Newport Primary School, Barnstaple

The Dark Mountain

In the dark mountain
Creepy-crawlies,
Dirty floor,
Dragons flying all over.

In the dark mountain
Dragons in tunnels,
Under spikes;
Silver walls
Under the dark floor.

In the dark mountain
Wobbly floors,
Wobbly sides,
Wobbly staircase.

Max Banbury (8)
Newport Primary School, Barnstaple

My Cat

My cat is a strange cat,
Charlie is her name.
She sleeps in the garage
To keep her out of the rain.

Every morning at half-past eight
She comes into the house,
She eats all her breakfast,
But wishes it was a mouse.

She loves jumping on handles
And opening up doors,
She cleans herself every day
And sharpens up her claws.

I love my cat very much,
She is my second best friend,
I will love my Charlie-cat
Until the very end.

Lewis Hall (8)
Newport Primary School, Barnstaple

Butterfly

B eautiful butterfly flying in the breeze,
U gly brown moth staring in the window.
T ouching a butterfly feels soft and gentle,
T ake a butterfly home and you are cruel.
E xcellent colours on a butterfly's wing,
R ed butterfly floating in the breeze of leaves,
F lying in the midnight breeze
L ike a bird with no beak and four wings.
Y ellow ones can be cabbage butterflies.

Shivon Burridge (8)
Newport Primary School, Barnstaple

Birthdays

Birthdays make you happy
They can be lots of fun
Whether you're a daughter
Or whether you're a son.

Mums and dads have birthdays too
Although they are much older
Mums try to hide their ages
And dads become more bolder.

It's nice to open cards and gifts
With family and friends
You7 have a party for them all
Which you never want to end.

Jelly, cake, bottles of pop
Music, games and laughter
You enjoy yourself and make a mess
Which mum will clean up after.

Charlie Sherborne (11)
Newport Primary School, Barnstaple

My Cats

My cats are warm, soft and fluffy
Long-tailed and bright-eyed
Sometimes huffy.

My cats are pretty
Sometimes lazy
And when they play
They go crazy.

My cats are fat
And they sleep a lot
I love my cats
An awful lot.

Naomi Straughan (9)
Newport Primary School, Barnstaple

The Mystical Forest

I saw in the distance a fearsome creature,
With reflecting scales all blue and red.
All around it the trees were singed.
From within the foggy wood, it reared its head.

As I crept forwards, I heard a thundering roar,
That came from the dingy wood.
Then whistling wind and rushing waters
Overwhelmed my ears where I stood.

I moved quietly to the edge of the forest
And smelled burning wood mixed with damp moss.
The creature stepped closer, I stepped back.
I thought my life was at a loss.

But as I looked at its face, I had a gentle feeling in me,
The creature seemed kind, but sad and alone.
I reached out and felt its scaly skin.
It felt warm to my hand, but then it let out a groan.

The poor creature was hurting, but its roar was so scary,
Everyone else had been too scared to go near.
I soothed its wound with moss from the ground
And left it in peace and no longer in fear.

Samuel Clarke (8)
Newport Primary School, Barnstaple

My Kitten

His coat is black and white
His fur is very silky
His eyes are green and black
His name is Jasper
He's very, very, very funny
He's very, very, very playful
He's joyful and fun
I got him for my birthday
His ears are pointy
His tail is black.

Melanie Thompson (8)
Newport Primary School, Barnstaple

My Hobby

Beyblading is my hobby.
I practise day and night.
No matter what my feelings,
I'd never miss a challenge.

My practise partner's Tom.
He's a real tough cookie.
But in a match against me,
I'd be ripped to shreds.

I try to specialise in speed.
I always check my blades.
I have a large collection of bits.
I'll always do my best.

Nicholas Shanley (10)
Newport Primary School, Barnstaple

Granny And Grandpa Blob

When I went to art club
We were told to draw our grandparents.
I drew them in fine detail
But teacher said,
'That's a blob, not your grandparents,
Do it nice and realistic this time.'
So I drew and drew as well as I could.
The picture looked really good
But I could tell there was something missing.
Eyes, mouth, nose, ears, they were all there.
When my grandparents picked me up
My teacher went to tell them about my good work
But, boy, did she have a surprise
When two blobs came to pick me up!

Sam Hui (11)
Newport Primary School, Barnstaple

Midnight

As the sun slowly drifts down and
Closes his eye,
I sit gazing out of the window
As he calls his last goodbye.
I wait and wait,
Until the stars appear,
Then I pause anxiously
For the moon to come near.
I stare up at the glistening stars
And listen to them all calling my name
As soft as a whisper
As my tears keep on falling.
The moon slowly emerges from
The darkness, and the silence ends
As the wolf howls.
Then at midnight I make my wish.

Rebecca Ellis (10)
Newport Primary School, Barnstaple

A Hare's Version

Bunny rabbits fluffy,
Carrot stalks green,
Old farmer's cabbages are better
Than they've ever been.
Beetroots purple,
Onions white,
I watch them grow,
Scarecrows don't give me a fright.
The apples are alright,
I've been well fed . . .
So watch out cos I'll be back, Old Farmer Fred!

Nicole McBride (10)
Newport Primary School, Barnstaple

Snow

I woke up in the morning
The winter's day was dawning
I looked out of the window and what did I see but snow.
The snow was pure white, oh what a sight!
I made a snowman in the snow
In his eyes there was a glow.
The day was ending, the sun shone out.
The snow was melting all about.

Rebekah Parsons (10)
Newport Primary School, Barnstaple

The Lost Kitten

I'm out in the wind and the cold
All I want is my mummy to hold.
I've lost my way, I'm on my own,
All my friends have gone home.
I'm roaming around the streets at night,
Lots of noise to give me a fright.
A bolt of lightning, thunder too,
Down comes the rain and soaks me through.
I see a dog that lives near me,
So I follow his steps to set me free.
I look in the distance, I see my house,
I run and run as if I were chasing a mouse.
Through the cat flap is where I bound,
Yes! I'm home! Safe and sound.

Abigail Tanton (11)
Newport Primary School, Barnstaple

Wind And Rain

I hate the wind and rain
Especially at night
It wakes me up too early
With a terrible fright.

Tapping on my window
Wind whistling through the trees
It's as bad as thunder and lightning
And starts a knocking of my knees.

When lightning flashes and thunder rumbles
It's like World War II outside
Suddenly a really loud *bang*
Shakes me up inside.

I wriggle further down
And pull the covers over my head
I can't wait until the morning
When I can get out of bed.

Jason Head (10)
Newport Primary School, Barnstaple

A Limerick About Nelly

There once was a girl who watched telly
Whilst wearing her green rubber welly

She never left the box
Not even to change her socks

So her feet became incredibly smelly!

Ashley Roberts (10)
Newport Primary School, Barnstaple

My Cat

Micky will sit around his bowl
Waiting for his food.
There is only one problem
He has an attitude.

Charlie will be outside
Trying to catch a bird.
Or if he isn't he'll be asleep
Not to be heard.

Micky is always in places
Where he shouldn't be.
In the bin, on the table
Or on the breakfast bar.

Charlie's always darting about
And tripping people up.
But he is a very cuddly cat
And likes to have a fuss.

Micky likes to take over the sofa
And stretch out as far as he can.
The only reason he does it
Is so nobody can sit down.

Micky and Charlie love each other
But sometimes like to fight.
If anyone gets in the way
They will probably get a bite!

Elisa Field (10)
Newport Primary School, Barnstaple

The Ghost

As I walked to the dark gate
It began to get very late.
Soon the moon was high above
In the sky like a silver dove.
The grey gate opened with a creak
I decided to take a little peek.
I couldn't help but to have a look
A few seconds it should have took.
I walked until I found a grave
A horrible feeling to my bones it gave.
I looked at the grave and my stomach tightened
I began to become very frightened.
I screamed as a silver hand came out of the ground
Then I heard a wailing sound.
I ran to the gate, which I never reached.

Jessica Poile (11)
Newport Primary School, Barnstaple

The Spider

Cunning-thinker,
Blood-drinker,
Sly-sneaker,
Evil-speaker,
Life-ender,
Death-sender,
Venom-drawler,
Sneaky-crawler,
Sharp-biter,
Vicious-fighter,
Pain-starter,
Quick-darter,
Fear-filler,
Swift-killer.

Eleanor Chamings (11)
Newport Primary School, Barnstaple

Cricket Is Fun

The bowler does lots of running,
over-arm he bowls the ball.
Will the batsman hit it or not?
I don't like bowling a lot.

As the batsman, you protect the wickets,
hope the bail won't be knocked off.
Hitting the ball far away,
how many runs can I get today?

As the fielder stands alone,
waiting to see if the ball will reach him.
'Hear that whistle,' coming my way,
arms up to catch it.
'Out!'

Aaron Milne-Redhead (10)
Newport Primary School, Barnstaple

My Dad

My dad was cool
We did lots of things together
Like riding bikes and flying kites
Especially in the summer.

We used to go on holiday
To a campsite by the sea
We always had a lot of fun
We have precious memories.

My dad is now in Heaven
I miss him very much
But at least I have photographs
And my special memories.

Matthew Wallin (11)
Newport Primary School, Barnstaple

Winter

Looking at the winter snow falling onto the ground,
Looking at the snowmen in the streets,
Looking at the birds shivering in the brown tree,
Looking at the brilliant white sky.

Tasting hot chocolate going down my throat,
Tasting cold air in my mouth,
Tasting my lovely hot dinner, yum,
Tasting my delicious ice cream after lunch.

Listening to the brilliant white snow banging on my window,
Listening to the TV muttering downstairs,
Listening to the chirping of the birds,
Listening to the fire crackling.

Jessica Loder (8)
Newport Primary School, Barnstaple

Penguins

Penguins, penguins
They are fun and they are cool
Penguins, penguins
Feel like a slippery wall
Penguins, penguins
Every shade of black and white
Penguins, penguins
Good for sliding on the ice.

Charli Dellaway (9)
Newport Primary School, Barnstaple

Winter

Icy fingers,
Trees dead,
A cool breeze on my head,
Silver sky,
Here I lie,
In the snow, here and there.

Slippery ice
Everywhere,
I would stay
In bed all night,
And I would
Never go outside
In the freezing air.

Ben Hardy (8)
Newport Primary School, Barnstaple

My Dog And I

He wakes me in the morning
With a rough and wet tongue.
He kicks me out of bed
To get the warmest spot.
He shares my cups of tea
And my breakfast too.
He waits for me when I come from school
And when I go to the loo!
We play along the beach and in the waves,
We truly are best friends.
It's how we spend our days,
My dog and I.

Danyelle Snell (10)
Newport Primary School, Barnstaple

Day And Night

The bird sits in her nest and bows down her head,
So does the daylight as it swaps with dark,
The moon, like a flower,
Follows the stars,
Pouring their sleep upon her head.
Out swoop the owls,
With silent delight,
Whilst dropping blessings upon her. Why?
Daylight stretches and rises steadily,
So does the bird as she opens her eyes.
The sun, like blossom,
Flowers its love.
Her petals lay themselves on the bird.

Lucy Hardy (11)
Newport Primary School, Barnstaple

My Subaru

My Subaru
Bright and blue
It's cool - my Subaru.

My Subaru
A posing machine
It's cool - my Subaru.

My Subaru
Shiny and clean
It's cool - my Subaru.

My Subaru
Fast and new
It's cool - my Subaru.

Samuel Pincombe (8)
Newport Primary School, Barnstaple

Foods

Foods, foods, tempting foods,
Which one shall I choose?
Dairy Milk or chocolate on toast?
Which one shall I choose?

Drinks, drinks, luscious drinks,
I don't know what to choose.
Hot chocolate or milkshake?
I like them both, you see.

Desserts, desserts, delicious desserts,
They're all nice we know,
Apple pie or sticky toffee pudding,
Mmmmm, which one shall I choose?
I love all foods, drinks and desserts,
But sometimes . . .

*I just don't know
What to choose!*

Charlotte Rushton (8)
Newport Primary School, Barnstaple

Fairy Magic

Fairies are my favourite things,
With pretty dresses and silver wings,
Fairies flying by,
How glittery they look.
Up so high, in the sky,
I can't believe my eyes.

Myah Field (8)
Newport Primary School, Barnstaple

I Wish I Was . . .

I wish I was a driver
Deadly and fast.

I wish I was an eagle
Noble and great.

I wish I was a killer whale
Silent and strong.

I wish I was a snake
Slippery and sneaky.

But I'd rather be a human
With my family and friends!

Jacob Harris (8)
Newport Primary School, Barnstaple

The Wind

The wind is roaring,
The wind is mighty,
The wind is breathtaking,
The wind is biting,
The wind is howling like a hungry wolf.

The wind is calm,
The wind is gentle,
The wind is smooth,
The wind is rippling,
The wind is nibbling
And whispering like a little mouse.

The wind is always changing.

Miles Kingsley (8)
Newport Primary School, Barnstaple

Seasons

Winter
Wind blowing,
Snow falling,
Rain lashing,
Hails beating.

Spring
Buds growing,
Snowdrops shooting,
Crocus peeking,
Daffodils growing.

Summer
Sun shining,
Sun burning,
Skin hot,
Water's cooling.

Autumn
Leaves falling,
Wind blowing,
Branches shaking,
Washing blowing.

Jason Tucker (11)
Newport Primary School, Barnstaple

The Sand

I love to go to the beach,
With crashing waves and the sand,
Building sandcastles, making moats,
Warm sand falling through my hand.

Bethany Westcott (8)
Newport Primary School, Barnstaple

Dolphins

Dolphins can jump,
Jump very high,
Sometimes they're pictured
In a sunset sky.

Dolphins can swim,
Swim underwater,
Very fast, more than they oughta.

Dolphins can splash,
Splash their tail,
Just the same as a humpback whale.

Dolphins can eat,
Eat lots of eels,
They certainly make very nice meals.

Rachel Elston (10)
Newport Primary School, Barnstaple

Football

Football is my favourite game,
I play it all the time.
I hope one day it will bring me fame,
Wearing number nine.

After school, down the park,
I play it with my buddy;
We play until it's really dark
And we are really muddy.

Man U is my favourite team,
I've been to see them play.
It would be my ultimate dream
To play for them one day.

Charlie Hedge (11)
Newport Primary School, Barnstaple

Animal Street

One day I went on a walk with my dog
We saw a rather large hedgehog.

We decided to follow it up the road
Then we saw a tiny, tiny toad.

We decided to follow them a little more
Then we saw a belching boar.

We saw a wall of iron
Behind it was a ferocious lion.

Down the hill of wavy grass
There was a lake of jumping bass.

Around the corner and down the pathway
Where some pigs on holiday.

Come on, let's run through the street
Twenty mooing cows we did meet.

Strolling through the field of hay
Harvest mice came out to play.

Hop, skip, jump, to the park
Three hissing cats made my dog bark.

Animals, animals everywhere
I even saw a monkey sitting on a chair.

Come on, Cassie, let's go home
I'll have a glass of Coke, you can have a bone.

Kurtis Hartnoll (10)
Newport Primary School, Barnstaple

Art

Art is my favourite thing to do,
I love drawing, colouring and painting too.
I can draw cartoons, people, cats and dogs,
I think I could even draw a few frogs.
I like making things, from mosaics to boxes,
I can draw an incredible picture of foxes.

Hannah Loder (11)
Newport Primary School, Barnstaple

The Hobbit

Hobbits aren't tall, they're very small
And they have curly hair on their feet.
They have lots of pantries full of food
Because their favourite thing is to eat.
They live in a hill with kitchens, bathrooms and more
And at the front of the hill is a green, shiny door.
In the bedrooms there are warm, cosy beds
And they clothes of yellow, green and red.

Kelly Featherstone (10)
Newport Primary School, Barnstaple

My Brother

Sometimes we play together
Sometimes we fight together
Sometimes we love each other
Sometimes we hate each other
But I don't care.
He's still my brother.

Hannah Sutton (8)
Newport Primary School, Barnstaple

My Chocolate World

I wish I lived in a chocolate world.
My house would be in Quality Street,
My garden full of Roses.
We would have Celebrations every day.

In the morning, when I wake,
I would have a Flake.
For my lunch and my dinner,
I would have a Snickers.

When the clock chimes eight
I would have an After Eight.
When it is time for bed
I love to cuddle my chocolate ted.
When it is time to close my eyes
I count the Magic Stars in the sky.

Jade Harris (8)
Newport Primary School, Barnstaple

Football

Football, football,
Is so great.
Football, football,
I play with my mate.
Football, football,
I kick it so hard
And hope not to get a red card.
Football, football,
No matter the weather.
Football, football,
I'll go for a header.

Liam Andrew (9)
Newport Primary School, Barnstaple

Football

F erocious tackles on the ground,
'O rrible refs who cannot decide . . .
O n a penalty . . . or was it a dive?
T aking chances and blowing some,
B oots that start off sparkling clean,
A nd finish very, very muddy.
L osing and winning depends how you play,
L uck plays its part at the end of the day.

T ime slowly ticking away,
E very player always counts,
A t every game, stakes are high,
M agnificent skill, lots by Okocha.
S ound of the whistle means ninety minutes are up.

Justin Southam (9)
Newport Primary School, Barnstaple

My Kitten, Sox

My kitten, Sox,
Is black and white,
She hunts for mice
All day and night.

She has a red collar,
She pounces and leaps,
She has a drink of milk
And goes to sleep.

She plays all day long,
She's really sweet,
She's the most purrr-fect cat
You will ever meet.

Charles Rogers (9)
Newport Primary School, Barnstaple

Wildlife

I like wildlife, wildlife is my thing,
When I go out walking
I like to hear birds sing.

Waiting in the dark
For the badgers to come out,
Must not make a sound,
Must not scream or shout.

Wildlife is my hobby, it's what I like to do
And maybe, when I'm older
I can help out at the zoo.

Matthew Pearson (9)
Newport Primary School, Barnstaple

Fright Night

It's a spooky, spooky night,
Be prepared to have a fright.
Hobbits in their hobbit holes
Are being visited by blind, black moles!

Witches in their creepy dens,
Black cats and spiders are their friends.
Be very careful where you go,
For there might be a zombie show!

Be afraid, shake with fear
Because all these things are getting near.
Turn around and run away,
Don't let the spooks get you today!

Jessica Smith (8)
Newport Primary School, Barnstaple

Four Seasons Of The Year

Spring
It's a surprise
When the flowers rise,
The frost dies
And the sun begins to shine.

Summer
The sun is rising
It is very surprising
The sun looks like gold
It is not cold.

Autumn
The wind is blowing
Nothing is growing
The rain starts to come down
All the leaves are brown.

Winter
It is very cold
The trees are bold
The frost comes out
And not many people are about.

Rebecca Benham (9)
Newport Primary School, Barnstaple

Honey The Hamster

Sleeps all day,
Awake all night.
Her favourite game
Is trying to escape.
Hope her lid's on tight!
She runs in her wheel,
Runs up the tube,
Nibbles her food,
She's a cool dude!

Jamie Shutt (9)
Newport Primary School, Barnstaple

People

People bowl and people hit,
People field in a game of cricket.
People dribble and people score,
People pass in a game of football.
People crawl and people win,
People dive when they are swimming.
People whack and people miss,
People serve in a game of tennis.
There are many sports under the sun,
Winning or losing . . .
It's all such fun!

Myles Payne (8)
Newport Primary School, Barnstaple

Mermaid

There's a mermaid swimming
In the blue sea.
She's combing her hair
And looking at me.
She waves, 'Hello!'
And I smile back,
She dives down below
And, like a Jumping Jack,
She's soon back.
In her hand she holds a shell,
A present for me,
Her newfound friend.

Gemma Bolsom (8)
Newport Primary School, Barnstaple

My Baby Brother

My baby brother has his milk,
And he's got skin just like silk.
My mum puts him in babygrows,
Fitting fingers, fitting toes.
He sometimes wakes up with a cry,
He's always hungry, I don't know why.
We sometimes play, then he is happy,
Unless he makes a dirty nappy!
Then to bed - he sleeps in a cot,
My new best friend I love a lot.

Thomas Roode (9)
Newport Primary School, Barnstaple

I Saw In The Sky

I saw in the sky
A charming little chaffinch
An evil-looking eagle
A jet-black jackdaw.

I saw in the sky
A murder of crows
A 'V' of Canadian geese
A pair of collared doves.

I saw in the sky
A red-breasted robin
A speckled house sparrow
A dazzlingly-coloured kingfisher

Siân O'Neill (8)
Newport Primary School, Barnstaple

Birds

Cheeky chaffinch, hungry crow
Singing blackbirds in a row
Tiny bluetits on a fat ball
Starving starlings eat it all.

Little sparrows like the peanuts
Thrushes looking for a tasty worm
Swifts and swallows fly above us
Robin redbreast feeds her young.

Popular peregrines waiting for mice
Puffing puffins really tired out
Kingfishers diving for their tea
Golden eagles really scare me!

Shane Prater (9)
Newport Primary School, Barnstaple

Favourite Things

I love . . .
Pretty pink in full bloom, red rose's dark
Peacefully play my clarinet
Those are some of my favourite things.

I love . . .
Honeycomb so creamy like a bee's house of sweetness
Those are some of my favourite things.

I love . . .
Chocolate chip ice cream and cool, cute Orlando Bloom
Those are some of my favourite things.

I love . . .
Lovely Lucky and smelly Smudge those are my dogs!
Lucky is big and Smudge is cute
Those are some of my favourite things.

Bernadette Wreford (11)
St John's CE Primary School, Totnes

Favourite Things

Jade green is a colour I like,
It makes me think of the sea with its sparkle of blue-green colour,
Dark elves, I like to collect,
I want to beat my brother at a game of figure battles.

I like running like a headless chicken.
I feel like I'm going to have a heart attack,
I like drawing dragons
I like making new things,
These are a few of my favourite things.

Joseph Trott (11)
St John's CE Primary School, Totnes

My Favourite Things

Sweet smelling chocolate that melts in your mouth,
Gorgeous, delicious and bad for your health.
Hoping that you will be able to pay,
For this delicious chocolate to eat all day.

Netball that's full of its talented players,
Jumping as high as elephant slayers.
Getting the ball right through the net,
Wishing their team hasn't lost just yet.

Dogs run around as they start to play,
Together at last on the farmyard hay.
Happy that the farmer cannot see,
That they've made the barn so very messy!

Beautiful blue is the colour of the sky,
A place where all birds can just fly.
Out of the wind and into space,
To start this magnificent wild goose chase.

Robyn McLellan (11)
St John's CE Primary School, Totnes

My Favourite Things

Rugby, the active game, taking all your anger out on the other team.
Liverpool, successful team together they will win the game.
Farming, I used to live on one
Playing and making dens in the hay barn
Ferrets, good hunters run around all day.
These are some of my favourite things.

Mark Nicholls (11)
St John's CE Primary School, Totnes

Favourite Things

Lemons, yellow bright
Glimmering in the hot sun
Lemons are the best

Linkin Park blowing
Tunes into my thick skull
Shouting their heads off

The blue sea gleaming
Blue my favourite colour
The blue sky shimmers

Pizza slices, yum
Pepperoni is my fave
Pizza yum, yum, yum

Portugal, sunny
Getting sunburnt, ow, ow
Lying in the sun

Bacon in the pan
I can't wait until it's fried
Sizzling, yum-yum.

Stephen Devlin (11)
St John's CE Primary School, Totnes

My Favourite Things

Clarinet
As I play, a smile appears on my face,
The music streaming out of the keyholes flowing gently to my ears.

Ice cream
Mint chocolate chip, blackcurrant and honeycomb.
All dripping down my face.

Watermelon
The water running down my chin,
As I bite into the succulent melon.

Smarties
Crunching the chocolate inside the coloured shell,
Then I fill my mouth with more.

Dogs
My dog's fur is a lion's mane
His teeth are as sharp as a blade.

Chocolate
Chocolate melting in the wrapper as I rub my tummy
Yum-yum.

Jasmine Moore (11)
St John's CE Primary School, Totnes

My Favourite Things

I like . . .
Dogs waiting at the door, the postman will be coming soon.

I like . . .
Cereal crunching in my mouth
The spoon clinks against the side of the bowl.

I like . . .
Going shopping with my mum, seeing everything I want!

These are a few of my favourite things.

Scarlett Fagan (11)
St John's CE Primary School, Totnes

My Favourite Things

Fish
As it tickles my skin while swimming through my legs.

Ice cream
Peppermint choc-chip running down my throat,
Melting away.

Bacon
Sizzling bacon sizzled in the slippery pan
As the smell trickles through the air.

Lemons
The lemon juice so sharp when I drink it,
It makes my face wrinkle up.

Science
With all the explosions and tests but the worst thing of all
I have to clear up the mess.

These are a few of my favourite things.

Matthew Edmonds (11)
St John's CE Primary School, Totnes

My Favourite Things

I love . . .
Animals, animals that growl!
Animals who wait for their fluffy toys.

I love . . .
Ice cream, ice cream dribbling down my cheek,
My favourite chocolate flavour.

I love . . .
Holidays, holidays where the sun beams on the sandy beach,
Waves crashing on the rocky rocks.

I love . . .
Sky-blue, sky-blue makes me feel calm and caring,

These are a few of my favourite things.

Abigail Robbins (11)
St John's CE Primary School, Totnes

Young Writers - Once Upon A Rhyme Devon & Cornwall

My Favourite Things

The colour of blue like the glistening sea,
Galaxy chocolate tastes heavenly to me
Leaping dolphins I could watch them all day
I love the holidays, no work, but play.

My dog Maisy, lazing in the sun
And with all my friends I have so much fun.
Sweet-butter popcorn is lovely to eat,
Dancing like a buttercup, with my feet.

Swimming like a shark, I break through the waves
And from the wall, the fierce sea shaves.
Munching and crunching, biscuits I love,
Silk, satin cushions as white as a dove.

Sweet smelling roses in full summer bloom
A wonderful, fresh and clean tidy room.
Together they can start to see,
How beautiful this place can be.

Fast cars that speed and especially Porches!
Wondrous, leaping and galloping horses
Evergreen meadows filled with dewed grass
And cute fluffy bunnies not least but last!

Rose Lewis (11)
St John's CE Primary School, Totnes

My Favourite Things

Eating ice cream
Because it tastes really yummy.
Football,
Practise to be the best.
Scary ghost stories,
Exciting crimes to solve.
Monkeys
Their hairy bodies swing from branch to branch.

These are a few of my favourite things.

Jamie Bevan (11)
St John's CE Primary School, Totnes

My Favourite Things

I love . . .
My hamsters, Squeak and Titch
With soft, silky fur.

I love . . .
My cats, Tigger and Poff.
Playful pleasure to have.

I love . . .
Cuddly Winnie the Pooh
When upset, I sit by him
And he cheers me up.

I love . . .
Dogs, playful running round
Like a mouse, very small.

I love . . .
Dolphins diving up and down
Jumping through the ocean waves.

These are some of my favourite things!

Rebecca Day (11)
St John's CE Primary School, Totnes

My Favourite Things

I love . . .
Ice cream, chocolate and toffee, melts in my mouth.

I love . . .
Cats, good friends, reliable and very trusting.

I love . .
Science, chemical reactions and the body.

I love . . .
Monkeys, swinging in the jungle, hairy bodies climbing in the trees.

Aaron Mead (11)
St John's CE Primary School, Totnes

My Favourite Things

Puppies
Puppies waiting for their food,
While licking loopy bones, with soft looking eyes.

Blue
The only colour that keeps me calm,
And waits for birds to fly up high.

Chocolate
Slimy slippery chocolate running down my sister's chin.

Orlando Bloom
Cute, cool Orlando Bloom, his eyes are like brown lion's skin.

Bunnies
Bunnies jumping up and down, while twitching tiny noses.

These are some of my favourite things.

Jemma Morris (10)
St John's CE Primary School, Totnes

My Favourite Things

Cornflakes in the morning
Soft, crisp and crunchy in the mouth
Watching television at night
Makes me feel funky
The colour black
Makes me feel like the night
My two nieces
Playing with Sophie and Rachel.

These are a few of my favourite things.

Aaron Spray (11)
St John's CE Primary School, Totnes

My Favourite Things

I love . . .
Pretty Palomino ponies cantering in the breeze,
Their tails swish as they sneeze!

I love . . .
Chocolate and toffee in my mouth,
As I walk down south.

I love . . .
The blue sea, lapping and jumping on the beach,
As I get bitten by a leach.

I love . . .
My kittens, Sugar and Spice
Eating cheesy rice.

I love . . .
Dogs, running across the sand
As a kangaroo bounces across the land.

I love . . .
Vanilla ice cream dripping down my sister's mouth,
As she looks in the mirror.

I love . . .
Horror movies, getting stuck in my mind
I go to bed and the images unwind.

These are a few of my favourite things.

Amber Bayldon (11)
St John's CE Primary School, Totnes

My Favourite Things

I love . . .
My bunny so furry and funny
Hopping round and round without a care in the world,
Oh my bunny isn't he lovely.

I love . . .
Netball, netball isn't it great
Here I am having fun
When I've finished
I'll have a bun.

I love . . .
Chocolate is delicious
I love it, I wish I always had it in my dish.

Elisha Pusey Gale (11)
St John's CE Primary School, Totnes

Jo Fisherman

Once there was a graveyard
An empty graveyard
An empty, lonely graveyard
And in that graveyard
There was a gravestone
An old dirty gravestone

Jo's grave
Fisherman's Jo's grave
Died 1910, Monday
Cold Monday

Jo Fisherman
St Mawes, Jo Fisherman
Home whistling Jo Fisherman
Disappeared into the cold, lonely night.

Alexandra Petrucci (10)
St Mawes Primary School, Truro

Small Ads

1940s teacher runs on school books and naughty children
Don't worry about the moaning and groaning that it makes
When you wake it up in the morning
Or the screaming it makes when it sees a kid
Sometimes you will need to give it a push to get it going
We are asking for anything just to get rid of her!

Lucy Goldsmith-Cannan (10)
St Mawes Primary School, Truro

Ghost Ship

Once there was a harbour
A weary harbour
A weary, spooky harbour
A harbour with no lights
And in that harbour was a ship
A ghost ship

In that ship was a door
A door with a rusty handle
A handle that turned your hands yellow
And in the door was a sword.

Aidan Shaw (10)
St Mawes Primary School, Truro

Small Ads

2000 low mileage sister
Economical as any other
Must mention, does need some attention
Streamlined, runs on milk, baby oil and gripe water
Serviced
Definitely needs rear wash/wipe
Only one owner
Not yet run in
Will swap for nothing.

Steven Green (8)
St Mawes Primary School, Truro

Small Ads

1930s granny
Bit slow when not in the mood
Needs oil, very rusty.
Can blow engine when starting up
Always takes a while to get going
Re-sprayed
Needs about sixty cups of tea a day
Cost - £10.25 or nine foreign coins
Not allowed to pay tomorrow - need money now.

Rosie Giles (9)
St Mawes Primary School, Truro

Small Ads

2001 low mileage sister,
Three years old, cheap to run
Must mention, does need some attention
Streamlined rear spoiler
Runs on milk, biscuits apples and water
Serviced.
Needs rear wash/wipe.
Only one owner, engine sometimes screams on frosty days.

Daisy Goldsmith-Cannan (7)
St Mawes Primary School, Truro

Small Ads

1950s teacher
Be nice or
She turns into a dragon
If she does
Give her a black coffee!
Going a bit grey
She runs a bit slow.

Kathrine Rosewall (10)
St Mawes Primary School, Truro

Small Ads

1962 Dad quite fast
Very rusty but only a few scratches
Nearly blind
Runs on cups of tea and biscuits

1960s teacher
Always screeching
Runs very slowly
Only a few grey hairs
Runs on naughty children
Will swap for anything

1920s granny, one of a kind
Runs on tea and biscuits
Very slow and needs hours to warm up
Plays 1940s songs
We are looking for anything under £5

1960s Mum a bit rusty
Bonnet always flies up
Especially when windy
Needs chrome treatment
Will swap for something unique
Sell for £1.15

1995 sister, very rusty
Needs to be fed on castor oil
No water except when washing
Will sell for anything or swap.

Lisa Thomson (10)
St Mawes Primary School, Truro

Small Ads

Miss Force
1950s teacher
Needs three or four repairs,
Loads of grey hairs.
Runs on gin and tonic
Needs rear wash/wipe.
In good clean, rust free state
Will swap for anything.

Jemima Hitchings (8)
St Mawes Primary School, Truro

Monday's Child

Monday's child is very tall,
Tuesday's child likes to climb a wall,
Wednesday's child has beautiful hair,
Thursday's child has ears like a bear,
Friday's child likes eating eggs,
Saturday's child has to beg,
But the child that was born on the Sunday
Is good and happy and likes to play.

Jane Elford (9)
Shute Community Primary School, Shute

The Dragon

The dragon is green
And very mean.
His fire is red
He has a scaly head.
His wings help him fly
He flies so high in the sky.
His tail is so long
He has a tongue.

Georgina Lamprill (9)
Shute Community Primary School, Shute

Christmas Counting Poem

One true God using His power
Two boys eat pudding, hour by hour,
Three girls pulling Christmas crackers,
Four sprigs of mistletoe, everyone gets smackers,
Five young children help put up the Christmas tree,
Six children look forward to Christmas with glee
Seven adults, play Christmas games,
Eight reindeers, being pulled by the reins,
Nine carol singers, singing in the snow.
Ten little robins, flying down low,
Eleven mince pies eaten by Auntie Nable
Twelve minutes later, there's none left on the table.

Robert James (9)
Shute Community Primary School, Shute

A Christmas Counting Poem

One St. Nicholas all jolly and red
Two snowmen outside with hats on their heads,
Three stars twinkling on the Christmas tree.
Four cards on the mantelpiece from my friends to me.
Five shiny angels touching the star.
Six shepherds travelling far.
Seven presents in a pile.
Eight mince pies made me smile.
Nine reindeer prancing over the rooftop.
Ten children eat so much they feel they could pop.
Eleven stockings hung by the fire.
Twelve cards from friends is what I desire.

Jedd Feldman (9)
Shute Community Primary School, Shute

The Day The Zoo Escaped

The day the zoo escaped . . .
The monkeys leapt out cheekily
The spiders scuttled out secretly
The tiger prowled out proudly
The rabbits bounced out loudly
The rats scurried out slyly
The cheetah raced out quickly
But the sloth just lazily hung around.

Alistair Rugg (8)
Shute Community Primary School, Shute

Blue

The glimpse of a whale's tail as it curls beneath the surface,
A sweet plum that's squidgy in my hand as I pick it up,
The pale sky slashed by plane trails,
The sea with seahorses dancing on the shore,
A rushing river racing me as I run to the bridge,
Eels wiggling in the glistening stream.

Daniel Fuzzard (8)
Shute Community Primary School, Shute

Autumn Is Born

Leaves like camouflage
Green and spotty
Curling and falling
Ash keys spinning
Tumbling down
Leaves going and coming
Tractors rumbling around,
Harvesting apples, plums and pears.

Matthew Morbey (9)
Shute Community Primary School, Shute

Squirrel

The squirrel is busy hunting for nuts.
Then scurrying across the forest ground
And rummaging in the leaves counting nuts.
The winter is coming quick, *hurry!*

Helena Buckley (8)
Shute Community Primary School, Shute

Light

My shape is a light shining bright all through the night.
It has a nice shade in beautiful red,
It's very well made and near to my bed.
It helps me see if I need a wee,
I switch off the light and say good night.

Martin Dixon (8)
Shute Community Primary School, Shute

Cutting Crops

Autumn has come
Farmers are happy cutting crops
At five in the morning
I think it's boring
I would rather stay in bed.

James Morbey (9)
Shute Community Primary School, Shute

What Is Pink?

What is red? A cherry is red.
Hungry mouths open and ready to be fed.

What is blue? The sea is blue,
Waves crashing down as the wind blew.

What is gold? Treasure is gold.
Hidden in a chest dusty and old.

What is pink? Tips are pink.
Holding a straw sipping a drink.

What is brown? Autumn leaves are brown.
Twisting and twirling and fluttering down.

What is green? The grass is green
Oh what a beautiful scene.

What is yellow? The sun is yellow.
Rising soft and mellow.

Dialah Roberts (8)
Shute Community Primary School, Shute

I Have A Photo Of My Cat

I have a photo of my cat playing with a plant.
Her grey fur glistens in the light.
Her shadow looks like a tiger about to pounce.
I don't know how she got on the table.
She leapt like a kangaroo.
I came home from school.
My cat came charging up to me.
We are in the front room.
Now she is lazing around,
And we play together.

Hannah Harris (10)
Sticklepath Primary School, Barnstaple

I Have A Photograph . . .

I have a photo of my nan
Sitting in her favourite armchair
Her eyes like two blue sapphires
Sparkling in the sun.
Her hand so gently holding me
Pressing me lightly to her neatly stitched cardigan
Is comforting me.

Last night I spoke to my nan on the phone
Her dog heavily panting
She started to stutter
Then started to slur
There was a sudden silence
She put the
Phone down.
It's like a cloud drifting apart
Like a biscuit crumbling
I will never see that happy face again.

Leanne Pemberton (10)
Sticklepath Primary School, Barnstaple

I Have A Photograph . . .

I have a photograph of my grandad holding me as a baby.
We are at my gran's house sitting on a red comfortable sofa.
I am facing my grandad asleep in his warm arms
Like a heater on full power.
Now I am older and my grandad is not here anymore
I will always look for my grandad photograph
And I will never forget it.

Ben Ferne (10)
Sticklepath Primary School, Barnstaple

I Have A Photograph Of . . .

I have a photograph of my nan's dog
Snuggling under a blanket with me
Trying to get to sleep.
He is as friendly as a pea letting you eat it.
His tan coloured and white stripped fur is as silky as a linen cloth.
He moves closer to me as if he is my baby brother,
Wanting to know about the rest of his life.

Today I will never see him again.
It's like he drifted away from one world to another
To lead a different life.
I feel sad as I walk down to his grave in my nan's orchard.
When I go home I look for the photo to remember
What fun we had together.

Libby Johnson (10)
Sticklepath Primary School, Barnstaple

I Have A Photo Of . . .

I have a photograph of my family,
Sitting in a stand,
Metal covering, shimmering behind us,
My cousin Chris sitting like the sunset,
We are celebrating his son's christening,
My dad and my brother in the front sparkling together,
My brother crying because he dislikes photos,
My other cousins leaning inside like a tree swaying in the wind,
Tonight when I speak to my cousins
Across the airways,
I will say "When are you coming down?"
And they'll say "Soon"
And I know that I will look for the photo
To remind me of the day I saw them
But that was then
And this is now.

Darrel Scales (11)
Sticklepath Primary School, Barnstaple

I Have A Photograph Of . . .

I have a photograph of some baby turtles
Just hatched out of the eggs,
Crawling round their box,
Carrying their shiny shells upon their scaled backs,
They are hungry for milk, so a person feeds them,
They are very lively even jumping on each other like crazy monkeys,
One of them is exploring the box, trying to climb over but can't,
It keeps on slipping off,
They can hardly see so they search for each other,
Their new shell sparkles in the flash of the camera
Like a bright green ruby.

Today I pay another visit, but this time they have grown,
They look at me like I'm a complete stranger,
As I get my camera out, they turn their faces,
I try to attract them, but they ignore me,
They plod around looking for the food they left
Last time they were fed,
Their eyesight is going, I can tell,
They are not lively, they are slow and weak like a droopy flower
Whatever happens I will always treasure
This photo of my favourite animal.

Samuel Downie (9)
Sticklepath Primary School, Barnstaple

I Have A Photo . . .

I have a photo of me playing football at Park School.
I am wearing my Man Utd strip proudly as I walk onto the pitch.
I resemble a Roman soldier marching to success.
A big day for me we had to win the final.

Connor Brayley (10)
Sticklepath Primary School, Barnstaple

My Photograph

I have a photograph of my brother Lewis
Snuggling up to my mum.
We are all around him.
He is smiling at the camera,
We are all in Woolacombe Bay.
Lewis has a red car in his hands,
His clothes are white and blue like the flag of Finland.
He is waiting for his first day at school.
Today he walked to school with me
Swinging his book bag side to side
And slurping his drink bottle annoying me.
With all the teachers giving him encouragement.
His behaviour has changed,
His temper is not so bad
But he still annoys me!

Amy Hale (11)
Sticklepath Primary School, Barnstaple

I Have A Photograph Of . . .

I have a photograph of my cat
Lying on a pool table
Playing with the snooker balls
Tensing up his muscles, his tummy full of meat
We're jealously laughing
Wishing we could be a cat
With a shimmering coat
Shining all through the year
While they lie on the floor relaxing

Now I see him lying on the floor
Waiting for someone to feed him,
No full tummy
Watching me dishing out the food
While he sits on the floor as bold as an elephant.

Sarah Henderson (10)
Sticklepath Primary School, Barnstaple

I Have A Photograph . . .

I have a photograph of my dad,
Playing football with me,
He is lying flat on the ground,
As still as ice after me scoring a goal,
Wearing blue denim jeans,
With a blue shirt, kangaroo logo
He looks like a blue sky on a sunny day,
I am wearing my complete Liverpool kit,
The red making me look like
A poppy field swaying in wind.
Today he will call from Peterborough,
And I can tell him all the things I like about him,
And tell him what I've done today,
When he says he is coming on Friday,
I would say, 'Yes' then 'Goodbye'
I will get all excited and look for the photo,
To remind me of the days we lived together,
When we could just do nothing,
Me and him on our own,
But that was then and this is now.

Toby Bennet (10)
Sticklepath Primary School, Barnstaple

I Have A Photograph Of . . .

I have a photograph of my mum and dad,
My brothers and me sitting on a chair together
Relaxing after a Christmas lunch
Excitedly waiting to open presents
Piled like lots of footballs.
I feel very happy to get the presents.
So does my brother, my mum and my dad.

Luke Manley (10)
Sticklepath Primary School, Barnstaple

I Have A Photo . . .

I have a photo of my kitten
Sitting on my sofa
My mum cuddling him
While my sisters argue childishly
Over who is going to hold him first.
His ginger fur is as bright as a glowing fire,
As his tail wiggles like a worm trying to get away,
His ears sticking out like flames from an oven.

But now he's lazy and is getting older by the minute,
His fur falling like feathers drifting from the sky,
Everyone forgetting him, like he never existed.

Ryan Tillman (10)
Sticklepath Primary School, Barnstaple

I Have A Photo Of . . .

I have a photo of a lion
Laying in the grass
His face has a smile on it
He grins at me
Like he wants to eat me for lunch
He couldn't get me
The high fence saved me
His giant paws came at the fence
Clawing and roaring
Trying to get me
I just stood there
Smiling at him.

Andrew Read (9)
Sticklepath Primary School, Barnstaple

I Have A Photograph . . .

I have a photo of my family sitting on an old sofa
Waiting for someone to turn the TV on.
My nan and grandad are at either end with seven of us between.
I share the care of my tiny baby cousin, with her brother.
She is in a tiny white Babygro.
She is as small as a baby ant.
She is a wonderful joy to everyone.

Today I saw my cousin in a car
With her mum and dad going to school,
I saw them smiling and waving at me.
Now my cousins are bigger I see them every day,
Every time I see them they always say hello!

Imogen Dawes (10)
Sticklepath Primary School, Barnstaple

I Have A Photo Of . . .

I have a photograph of my best friend, aged ten
Playing with me
And his other buddies
On the apparatus at my old school.

He is trying not to touch the floor.
It is difficult for him
Because people are pushing him around or off.
He is my best friend at my old school.

Oliver Winsor (10)
Sticklepath Primary School, Barnstaple

I Have A Photo . . .

I have a photo of my great-gran
Sitting down with all her grandchildren,
Laughing as her youngest grandchild smiles in a sunny sort of way.
My great-gran is wearing a flowery dress
Like a summer garden in the night and a green cardigan.
We are at my cousin's house,
My great-gran's eyes sparkling into the camera.
Now she still calls on Fridays,
Arguing what time she and my mum should go shopping
'10am,' my mum says.
I always think of her at school,
What it is like for her day after day alone in her house,
Watching TV and eating her shortcakes
With her golden angel glasses on,
A woman who once had a life of happiness and still does.

Scott Paddon (11)
Sticklepath Primary School, Barnstaple

I Have A Photo Of Me On A Horse

I have a photo of me on a horse
Riding along a bumpy old road,
Splashing through water, cooling us down in the red-hot sun.
We stop for a rest,
The horse drinks from the deep, slow running river.
I had a drink, refreshing me like a warm bath.

James Reeves (10)
Sticklepath Primary School, Barnstaple

I Have A Photograph Of My Sister

I have a photograph of my sister
On a trip to Disneyland, Paris,
Standing on a wall beside lush green grass.
Her hunk of brown hair in two pigtails with sparkly bobbles,
That shimmer in the spotlight of the sun's beam.
Her colourful dress stands out
Like a card in a funeral of grieving people.
A crowd of tourists and travellers flashing their camera lenses
At this star in the spotlight of the sun.

Now I relive the excitement that I felt when I took the photo.
The tension is killing me, but still it is overwhelming
As I wait for that day that seems years away.
My sister is not upset that the spotlight is no longer on her,
But on my mother and father like a hawk
As people come down to visit like flies on a wounded deer
And the wedding cards pile on our fluffy doormat.

Jade Connell (11)
Sticklepath Primary School, Barnstaple

My Photograph

I have a photo of me as a baby in someone's arms.
We are all in scruffy clothes except me.
In my bright pyjamas and warm, soft blanket.
My mum and dad are at the side, hot cups of tea in their hands.
My grandad sitting on the ice-cold step, with me in his hands,
A soft petal on my warm blanket feeling safe,
My nan telling my cousin off for biting her toenails,
My great Nanny Baker in her best clothes,
My aunty at the very back in her snowy-white jacket.
As for the rest I only know them in the photo.

Hannah Baker (10)
Sticklepath Primary School, Barnstaple

My Photograph

I have a photo of my nan in a Butlin's chalet.
My grandad sits next to her on a comfortable sofa.
They look at the camera with smiles on their faces.
My nan is wearing a summer dress prettier than the world could be,
But my grandad's clothes blur in the background.
My nan is wearing a 24ct gold necklace around her neck.

The locket around her neck.
The locket she had when my mum was little.
The locket I played with when I was little.
The locket that has a photo of my nan and grandad in.
The locket, so special to me.

Today my nan rings my heart from her grave
Telling me how important life is and to always stay strong.
Before I say goodbye to look for her locket.

Rosie Joslin (10)
Sticklepath Primary School, Barnstaple

I Have A Photograph Of . . .

I have a photograph of me on my quad bike.
In the summer when the sun was shining.
Dad and me enjoying ourselves.
In grandma's bumpy camp field.
My white, grey, black and bright green quad bike has three seats.
One on the back, one on the front.
And a comfortable one in the middle for the driver.
I ride my quad bike,
Made for me by my dad, on my own.
I still ride the same quad bike.
A year after my dad made it for me.

Annabel Roseveare (9)
Sticklepath Primary School, Barnstaple

I Have A Photo Of . . .

I have a photograph of me sitting on the floor.
With three cousins and three friends.
Unwrapped birthday presents in front of me.
I have a plastic brightly coloured shaped teddy bear xylophone
One of my cousin's blowing into a plastic red trumpet
We are all full up from party food
Hair pulled to one side
Squeezing my hands with excitement
My friends and family look into the camera
Last night I spoke to my cousins over the phone
From their comfortable, warm home
We talked about my first birthday and the photo we had
We said we all miss each other, my little cousin nearly cried
We all comfort one another
We discuss what we're gonna do when we see each other
We all comfort one another
We chat about who else was at the party
And that we never saw them ever again.

Shannon Longmuir (10)
Sticklepath Primary School, Barnstaple

I Have A Photograph Of . . .

I have a photo of my great nan sitting on her king-size bed.
She is wearing her teddy bear PJs while eating a warm sausage roll
Her PJs are red, yellow and brown.
She changes while in her cotton nightwear.
Her brightness fading into the night,
Like a star turning away.

Andrew Harris (10)
Sticklepath Primary School, Barnstaple

Naming A Baby

So hard to choose your favourite name,
Always stuck because none are the same.
I might be here all day,
Everyone is different in their own way.
I think she looks like an Amy or a Naomi,
She could be called Lucy, meaning light,
But there is always Zoe, which sounds quite nice.
I can't forget Kate.
I've got it - how about Abby?
Yes - she looks like an Abby,
Definitely Abby . . . oh, no, it's not right!

Lucy Bailey (11)
Stratton Primary School, Bude

Space Marine

S hining guns in war,
P eople going into battle
A ttacking the opponents
C ommanding people to fire
E ntire troops marching in unison.

M achine guns firing everywhere,
A rmies in formation
R apid shots repeating
 I solated on the battlefield
N oisy atmosphere
E xplosions creating craters in the ground.

James Wharton (11)
Stratton Primary School, Bude

The War Of The Ocean

Night engulfs the shore,
The moon highlights the rock pools,
Like a spotlight searching.
The water is still and shimmering,
Like diamonds, glistening in the moonlight.
Suddenly the water rises up,
A colossus of a wave sieges the cliffs,
Assaulting the rock face.
Then the wave shatters,
The rock face braces for impact,
As another wave approaches . . .

Jack Pickard (10)
Stratton Primary School, Bude

Zoë

Wrapped up in a blanket
Zoë our little sister.
Number nine in our family
Felt so light like the little bundle was empty
Smooth skin, her hand grips my finger.

All of us play with her,
Play walking and play talking.
She gurgles and burbles
She laughs at our jokes.

Zoë is the best baby in the world!

Tom Sillifant (10)
Stratton Primary School, Bude

Spring

Sprouting flowers everyday,
Bluebells covering the forest floor,
Fields hardly green any more,
Turning gold from dandelions,
Every plant growing back for spring,
Golden daffodils growing high,
Trying to touch the light blue sky,
Trees growing their green leaves back,
Giving off a shadow which is dark and black,
Spring can't go on forever you know,
In a few months it will be summer,
But make the most of the months of spring,
So let's look after our beautiful countryside,
It's worth treasure chests of diamonds and gold
Save our views of trees and flowers,
Don't let it go to waste, let it last forever.

Thomas Marlow (11)
Stratton Primary School, Bude

Farm Animals

I am a pig
All pink and heavy
Oinking, grunting
In the sty.

I am a cow,
All black and white
Mooing and munching
Through day and night.

I am a sheep
All covered in wool
Baaing and nibbling
Till I am full.

Laurence Haydon (11)
Stratton Primary School, Bude

ABZ

A t school

B ullies are not so cool

C harlie can't face them

D anielle pretends she's ill

E ric just laughs - he said he didn't know how upset people get

F rankly no one believes him

G rampa says ignore them

H ow do you do that?

I can't ignore bullies, can you?

J ulie got punched in the face today

K aren is the meanest pig

L ook at them and think:

M y family are happy - what about theirs?

N o one knows about

O llie's family, or

P etra's.

Q ueens of the school don't have to be cool;

R ebecca's kind

S ophie gives you crisps and last of all

T alan cleans up after PE

U nder all this writing you could help

V ery much, by reading the rest of this poem

W hy can't bullies be normal? It's just like

X ylophones can't talk

Y ou can make the world a better place

Z zzzz.

Shannon O'Neil (10)
Stratton Primary School, Bude

Bullies

B ack stabbing people who try to hurt you.

U nder the old battered roof of the bike shed you head for safety until home time.

L ittle bits of soggy paper hit the back of your neck.

L ying friends telling your biggest secrets, taking your belongings when you're not around, thinking it's funny.

I t's midday they throw your food across the hall, say they wouldn't do such a thing and not admit to it.

E normous amount of homework normally no problem for you, but not today.

S o you tell a teacher what's been happening and now they bully you even more, ask you things like 'Why did you tell? You get us into even more trouble.'

Emily Horstmann (10)
Stratton Primary School, Bude

Netball

It's Thursday and it's the end of school,
I'm playing netball and our team rule,
I sprint, shout and wait for the ball,
And as I grab it, I trip and fall,
We all pass it in a line,
I've run into the semi-circle just in time,
Determined to score a goal in the hoop,
Get it in and we all go whoop,
We switch ends getting ready to play,
I've scored another goal, we all cry hooray,
The final whistle goes, and we've won two-nil,
It's been such a great day, our team are brill,
I'm going to the comprehensive very soon,
To join their team I'd be over the moon,
I'm looking forward to going to the school,
And I bet the team will be really cool.

Kelly Simpson (11)
Stratton Primary School, Bude

Walking Around Town

Walking around town
Who do you go with?
Mates, boys, families?
In a group, just one friend?
A couple of boys, your mum, your dad?

Walking around town
Where do you go?
Shops, cafes, parks?
Visit the arcades, look for just one thing?
Go to eat, hang around the coolest streets?

Walking around town
When do you go?
Before lunch, after evening?
In the morning, just for a bit?
The whole afternoon, early night?

Walking around town
Why is it fun?
Buy things, get out the house, see mates?
Need a new top, just look around!
Want to get shot of your little brother?
Join your friends;
Walking around town.

Alice Weghofer (11)
Stratton Primary School, Bude

SATS

Big words, small words
Make me dizzy
My brain feels like wobbly jelly
Butterflies tickle my tummy
But the multiplication keeps me busy
My eyes hurt and my fingers ache
The pencil burns and it breaks
But in the end it's really just a piece of cake!

Ben Stanbury (11)
Stratton Primary School, Bude

Bullies

They snatch your bag and wallet
And laugh at you in your face
They tease you about your greasy hair
And you feel like you're a disgrace

They threaten you with objects
And trip you up when you walk past
But you know you've got to go away
So you run away very fast

But it can be stopped
Building up your self-esteem
Can make you say
'Stop, I've had enough!'
They may immediately stop
Or they might keep saying stuff

If they carry on
Try and re-build your confidence
Then go to a teacher
They can make the bullies see sense

But remember
Bullies are probably jealous of you
You're obviously more stronger
Than they are too.

Rachael Cuthbertson (11)
Stratton Primary School, Bude

The Sea

As the royal-blue water smashes and breaks,
With every leap the dolphins make,
On the crest of the waves white horses stride,
Galloping, manes furling of pride,
The shimmering water mirrors the sky,
As the crimson sun begins to die.

Sacha Perring (11)
Stratton Primary School, Bude

Alcohol

Alcohol is addictive.
It destroys your liver.
It makes you drunk.
Wobbling and groaning as they
Stagger along the street.
He appeared in the window and gave me a fright
His face was red and spotty and his eyes looked furious
And then he carried on wobbling up the road.
Think before you drink!

James Hyde (11)
Stratton Primary School, Bude

Clothes

C an never decide what to wear,
L ook, that top would look stunning with those trousers,
O h, Jamelia is wearing a top just like this one on the cover of her
new album,
T hat skirt would look lovely with that T-shirt.
H ow I tire of opening that door and having to chose what to wear,
E verything has something it could go with,
S ee how hard it is to decide!

Naomi Gillgren (11)
Stratton Primary School, Bude

Rainbow

R ose as a red rose on a romantic dinner,
A gapanthus are as sparkly midnight space,
I ris's purple as the sunrise in the morning
N arcissi yellow as the stars in the midnight sky,
B luebells shimmer and shine covering the forest in a blue sheet,
O xeyedasies glitter and glisten in the moonlight smudging snow
on the ground,
W hite dahlias in bunches looking like clouds in the sky.

Lucy Regan (10)
Stratton Primary School, Bude

Best Bud

Having a best bud is cool to have around,
Laughing, having fun in the school playground,
Share your secrets, share your dreams,
Hoping my best bud will get in the hockey team,
Hanging out like going to town,
Outside the classroom messing around,
Going to parties, meeting new friends,
Sunbathing at the beach wishing the day will never end,
Shopping, looking at the latest clothes,
Talking about piercing our noses,
Trying out hairstyles on each other,
Putting new CDs on, one after another,
Skipping, playing with the hoops at school,
Making sure we follow the rules,
Share your secrets, share your dreams,
Our friendship is like a flowing stream.

Holly Lloyd (11)
Stratton Primary School, Bude

Riding The Motorbike

Clutching my dad
Steering the bike through the woods
Stopping when we get to a pheasant feeder.

Splashing through the streams
Making waves either side
A pheasant waddles into view.

It spots us, it then starts to run, then it flies squawking
Above our heads.

Michael Chidley (11)
Stratton Primary School, Bude

Warhammer

W ar and destruction never knowing when to stop killing innocent
    life forms.
A ttacking and destroying the undefeated.
R abid kroot hounds ripping people and life forms to shreds.
H umans and innocent beings blown up by tau gun shots.
A rmageddon one of the many planets torn apart by war
    and cratered.
M ashing, the great unclean one destroys the chaos champion.
M any towel warriors getting destroyed no one caring, just fighting for
    the planet.
E nemies and friends equal to each other's powers and
    magic abilities.
R aging the no-man's-land in search of precious items and land
    to conquer.

Jack Gardner (11)
Stratton Primary School, Bude

Feelings!

F orever you want to be with your best friend.
E ven when you fall out,
E very time you close the friendship gate for a new one to open you
    have to wait and wait and wait,
L ooking really, really glad though you're actually really sad,
I f only I had a brother to stick up for me,
N o one ever listens to me so I feel angry,
G oing's getting extra tough,
S o I'm feeling ever so rough!

Amy Clarke (11)
Stratton Primary School, Bude

The Sea

On the rocky bay of Clovelly
The sea crashes against the cliffs
Cliff faces on the shore
Gazing out to sea
Seagulls constantly calling
While keeping their eyes on their young
The cliffs are struggling to face the eroding force of the sea
Slowly and silently, the sea is creeping in.

Ryan Curtis (11)
Stratton Primary School, Bude

Hope And Hate

H ands of fire destroy you.
A narchy reins on a throne of blood.
T ainted life corrupted by evil.
E verybody hates.

H appiness and laughter all around.
O verall joy is given.
P enetrating dark thoughts and evil.
E ternal love brings hope.

Michael Gliddon (10)
Stratton Primary School, Bude

Birds

In the garden I sit waiting for the sound of a bird calling.
Tall birds, small birds from different countries.
Birds have different colours and shades,
Birds can peck, scratch and bite.
When they are flying they swoop down for their prey.
They build their nests high in the trees,
Above in the bright green leaves.
Their babies grow and leave their home.
And through the skies they start to roam.

Lee Raper (11)
Stratton Primary School, Bude

Why?

What is the point in poems?
They're just words that rhyme
I don't know why
We have to do them
They're just a waste of time.
My pencil keeps breaking -
It's very frustrating.
Can't think what to say.
Let us go out to play!

Richard Herzog (11)
Stratton Primary School, Bude

Daydreaming

27+ . . . football I want to go into strike
27+12 = . . .
We're ending the season soon
'Charles!'
'Sorry Miss, 27+12=39
78+99 is . . .'
Last match on Tuesday
'Charles hurry up!'
78+99=177
Playing last year's winning team
Number 4-78+. . . = 300 . . .
Attacker coming towards me, the ball at his feet
'Charles . . . wake up at the back!'
78+222=300, done!

Charles Gifford (11)
Stratton Primary School, Bude

Warhammer

Painting a model,
It seems to take a lifetime,
Watching it as you slowly bring it to life,
Finally finished,
Send it into battle,
Control the great armies of the Imperium,
Or bring death to the false emperor with the evil hordes of Chaos,
A glorious victory,
A fatal defeat,
This is the world of Warhammer,
All packed away in a few small models.

Josh Hearn (11)
Stratton Primary School, Bude

The Polar Bear

Inside the polar bear's white fur, the never-ending snow.
Inside the never-ending snow, the polar bear's foot.
Inside the polar bear's foot, the orange horizon.
Inside the orange horizon, the polar bear's eye.
Inside the polar bear's eye, the blackness of the breathing holes.
Inside the blackness of the breathing holes, the seal's breath.
Inside the seal's breath, the polar bear's jaws.
Inside the polar bear's jaws, the volcanoes of blood.
Inside the volcanoes of blood, the red snow.
Inside the red snow, the polar bear's white fur.
Inside the polar bear's white fur the never-ending snow.

Taylor Bond (10)
The Grove Primary School, Totnes

The Ocean

If I was at the ocean
All I would see is
Miles and miles and miles of the ocean.

The sun was setting
All the dolphins were jumping
Children were splashing and jumping.

The sun went down
It all went black
The moon came up
People couldn't believe their eyes
The moon was as bright as one million lights altogether
You would need maybe two pairs of sunglasses or more.

You couldn't drag yourself away.

Almost morning
The sun came up
People awake
They go in the ice-cold sea hoping something would happen
And all movement stopped.

Emily Laffan (11)
The Grove Primary School, Totnes

Barn Owl

On a branch quietly sitting
Watching, waiting ready to swoop
He sees the mouse and makes it move.

Eyes wide, quietly,
Watching, waiting ready to fly.
Over the town in the still
Of the night,
Stars twinkling, moon shining bright.

Ben Hoare (11)
The Grove Primary School, Totnes

Two Greedy Children

Two greedy children, eating all the food
Their stepmother said 'Enough! They're rude!'
She tried to leave them in the woods, free to roam
But the brats ran back to their small step-home
So she tried once again - successful today
The kids ran along, screaming 'Hey!'
Until they found a sweetie house
And ate it like a giant mouse.
Out came the owner - told them off
'You naughty things my house to scoff!'
She tried to put them in the cooker
But the children pulled and bashed and shook her.
Now finally she has succeeded
People like that are just not needed!

Joe Sutton (10)
The Grove Primary School, Totnes

Yeti

Inside the yeti, the dangerous eye.
Inside the dangerous eye, a hot ball of fire.
Inside the hot ball of fire, the sharp claw.
Inside the sharp claw, a rusty bone.
Inside the rusty bone, a black spider.
Inside the black spider, a blade of grass.
Inside the blade of grass, food for ants.
Inside the food for ants, so the circle begins again.

Alex Bayley (10)
The Grove Primary School, Totnes

Nightmare

Black, deserted thoughts surround this hidden place,
The thorns of Hell cut the skin, of Heaven's innocent face,
Lost words whisper, forgotten by life outside,
The air, so thick, it digs at your flesh until your heart has died,
Evil eyes stare in the darkness, then take away a life,
Truth is consumed within a second, nothing can survive,
A river of blood flows continuously, shrouding all hearts,
The flame of anger will rise again, ripping souls apart,
Something's moving, shrilling voices
Run or die, no more choices,
A light,
A calming voice,
It's gone.

Bryony Doyle (10)
The Grove Primary School, Totnes

Swift But Deadly

Inside the fox's tail, a swift breeze blows.
Inside the swift breeze, the fox's eyes look upon its prey.
Inside the fox's eye the sun beats down.
Inside the sun the claw attacks.
Inside the claw the river of blood flows.
Inside the river of blood flows.
Inside the river of blood the fang lays stained red.
Inside the fang the mountains glisten.
Inside the mountains the fox's tail.

Ben Watkins & Harry White (11)
The Grove Primary School, Totnes

The Snake

Inside the snake's eye, an evil fire,
Inside the evil fire, the snake's tongue,
Inside the snake's tongue, a red sea,
Inside the red sea, the snake's deadly venom,
Inside the snake's deadly venom, a plain of scales,
Inside the plain of scales, the snake's land of ice,
Inside the snake's land of ice, a cold heart,
Inside the cold heart, the snake's dagged fangs,
Inside the snake's dagged fangs, a pair of mountains,
Inside the pair of mountains, the snake's eye.

Anthony Butts (10)
The Grove Primary School, Totnes

The Leopard!

Inside the leopard's paw, the inky sunset,
Inside the inky sunset, the leopard's spots,
Inside the leopard's spots, the night's stars,
Inside the night's stars, the leopard's eye,
Inside the leopard's eye, the untouched sky,
Inside the untouched sky, the leopard's fangs,
Inside the leopard's fang, the dark cave,
Inside the dark cave, the leopard's breath,
Inside the leopard's breath, the raging winds,
Inside the raging winds, the leopard's prey,
Inside the leopard's prey, the silent forest,
Inside the silent forest, the leopard's heart,
Inside the leopard's heart, the frosty ground,
On top of the frosty floor, the leopard's paw.

Sophie Maunder (11)
The Grove Primary School, Totnes

Inside A Bear!

Inside the bear's cold heart, the silver blood runs free.
Inside the silver blood that runs free, lays the bear's tongue.
Inside the bear's tongue, the ragged valley of stones.
Inside the ragged valley of stones, the bear's overturned stomach.
Inside the bear's overturned stomach, the river of chances.
Inside the river of chances, the bear's knife shaped claw.
Inside the bear's knife shaped claw, the rage of fire.
Inside the rage of fire, the fish's scale.
Inside the fish's scale, the bear's nose.
Inside the bear's nose, the glint of the moon.
Inside the glint of the moon, the bear's leg.
Inside the bear's leg, the icy ground.
Inside the icy ground, the bear's arm.
Inside the bear's arm, the river that flows free.
Inside the river that flows free, the bear's cold heart.

Sophie Chambers (11)
The Grove Primary School, Totnes

Scaresome Looks

Inside the bear's scaresome looks, lies the river that never flows.
Inside the unflowing river, the bear's paw.
Inside the bear's paw, the powdery snow.
Inside the powdery snow, the bears fang.
Inside the bear's fang, the blood of a thousand men.
Inside the man's blood, the bear's roaring voice.
Inside the roaring voice, the howling wind of the forest.
Inside the howling wind, the bear's beating heart.
Inside the beating heart, the poisoned lake.
Inside the poisoned lake, the bear's scaresome looks.

Joe Bryon-Edmond (11)
The Grove Primary School, Totnes

Inside The Bear

Inside the bear's growl, the ferocious wind,
Inside the ferocious wind, the bear's fur,
Inside the bear's fur, the free grass,
Inside the free grass, the bear's foot,
Inside the bear's foot the stony moor,
Inside the stony moor, the bear's tongue,
Inside the bear's tongue, the deer's blood,
Inside the bear's blood, the bear's claws,
Inside the bear's claws, the frozen mountain,
Inside the frozen mountain, the bear's heart,
Inside the bear's heart, the open plain,
Inside the open plain, the bear's growl.

Samuel Farthing (10)
The Grove Primary School, Totnes

Best Friends

Would a best friend
Go to a party
Without you?
Mine did.

Would a best friend
Go in someone else's house
Without you?
Mine did.

Would a best friend
Go to a football
Match without you?
Mine did.

Sorry I didn't let you come to the party.
Sorry I didn't let you come in the house with me.
Sorry I didn't let you come to the football match.
'Friends?'

Daniel Bovey (11)
The Grove Primary School, Totnes

Three Billy Goats' Revenge

Once upon a story rhyme
Somewhere far away
Three Billy goats gruff
Graze in a field all day

Very near by
Stood a rickety bridge
Where a troll so mean
Under there he lived

One fine day
The three goats said
'We should get rid of that troll
And replace him instead!'

They huddled together
And thought of a plan
'A gun should do it'
Cried Billy goat gran

She loaded the gun
The troll ducked down
Bang, bang, bang
Get out of town

That was it
The troll had gone
The three goats chuckled
Hip, hip, hooray!

Abigail Carthew (11)
The Grove Primary School, Totnes

The Limerick Of John

There was a young boy called John,
Who loved to play with a bomb,
He didn't realise,
That it was alive,
After that he didn't live long.

Danny Martin (10)
Threemilestone Primary School, Truro

A Day At Chapel Porth Beach

It's a blustery noon at Chapel Porth beach,
In the midst of the January weather,
It's a lovely day, the gorse is yellow,
And buds are forming on heather.

As I stand on top of the rocky cliff,
I look down at the roaring sea,
Galloping white horses charge to the shore,
And the sea spray showers me.

As the tide sneaks in towards the cliff,
Another wave begins,
And as I stare into the swirling ripples,
Out slides a shiny fin.

The fin disappears back into the sea,
I smile as I watch it go,
Another wave bursts, spray shoots in the sky,
Every colour of the rainbow.

The ocean rumbles, the waves fall in,
An earthquake, could it be?
The waves curl like an open mouth,
I hear the whisper of the sea.

As we walk on down the stony path,
We come to an old dark mine,
I peer inside, it's dark and wet,
The walls are covered in grime.

Behind the mine is a grassy green hill,
On it, a gorgeous hedgerow,
Right at the top is a carpet of white,
Where the daisies sit straight in a row.

The sun starts to set, the sky dims it's light,
For now it is nearly the start of the night.

Cara Searle (11)
Threemilestone Primary School, Truro

The Camping Trip

(Based on 'The Jabberwocky' by Lewis Carrol)

'Twas Sunday and silly family,
Sat around the fire yelling to each other.
All mimsy was old man silly,
And young lady silly was feeling grim.

'Beware the grizzly bird my son
His beak that pecks, its talons that catch.
Beware the eagle bear, and shun
The evil earring snatch.'

He took his stick and marshmallow in hand
Slowly it cooked over the fire.
So rested he by the carved out tree,
And sat awhile in no thought.

And as in toughish no thought he sat,
The grizzly bird with wings of flame.
Came killing through the trees
And pecked as he came.

He didn't think too fast as he flew past,
The well placed branch went slickers-mack!
He left him stunned and with the dead
Bird he went galumphing back.

And has thou got the answers, master silly
Oh frabjous day they chortled in their joy.

'Twas Sunday and the silly family,
Sat around the fire yelling to each other.
All mimsy was old man silly.

Ross Pascoe (10)
Threemilestone Primary School, Truro

Jabberschooly

(Based on 'The Jabberwocky' by Lewis Carroll)

'Twas Wednesday and the naughty boy,
Did dig and make holes in the gym.
All unhappy was Miss Hannabrove,
And Mr Grast was grim.

'Beware the maths man, my friend,
His sums that snarl, his co-ordinates that catch!
Beware the deputy bird and shun
The evil eggs that hatch.'

He took his destroyable pen in hand,
Long time his problems end he sought.
So rested he by the girls lavatory,
And sat a while in thought.

And in a toughest thought he sat,
The maths man with eyes of sums,
Came calculating through the entrance door,
And subtracted as he came.

He thought real fast as he went right past,
His well placed soap went slipperysmack.
He left him stunned, with his sums,
And he went galumphing back.

'And have you got the answers, Jackie?'
'Definitely Sir,' beamed the naughty boy.
For a change he got them right
And partied with lots of joy.

'Twas Wednesday and the naughty boy,
Did dig and make holes in the gym.
All unhappy was Miss Hannabrove,
And Mr Grast was grim.

Carly Maker (10)
Threemilestone Primary School, Truro